THE HISTORY OF ROCK 'N' ROLL

RITCHIE YORKE

THE HISTORY OF ROCK 'N' ROLL

EYRE METHUEN

London

(prepared in association with CHUM Ltd.)

Copyright © 1976 Super Grease Ltd. and Methuen Publications

All rights reserved. No part of this publication may be reproduced, stored in a retrieval system or transmitted in any form or by any means, electronic, mechanical, photo-copying, recording or otherwise, without the prior written permission of Methuen Publications, 2330 Midland Avenue, Agincourt, Ontario, Canada.

First published in Great Britain 1976
by Eyre Methuen Ltd.
11 New Fetter Lane, London EC4P 4EE

ISBN 0-413-37640-0

Cover design by John Kosh

Printed and bound in the United States of America

1 2 3 4 5   80 79 78 77 76

CONTENTS

Acknowledgments 7
The Development
of Popular Music 9
Introduction 11
Chapter 1 / 1955   13
Chapter 2 / 1956   18
Chapter 3 / 1957   23
Chapter 4 / 1958   28
Chapter 5 / 1959   34
Chapter 6 / 1960   39
Chapter 7 / 1961   45
Chapter 8 / 1962   50
Chapter 9 / 1963   56
Chapter 10 / 1964   98
Chapter 11 / 1965 104
Chapter 12 / 1966 110
Chapter 13 / 1967 116
Chapter 14 / 1968 123
Chapter 15 / 1969 130
Chapter 16 / 1970 136
Chapter 17 / 1971 142
Chapter 18 / 1972 148
Chapter 19 / 1973 156
Chapter 20 / 1974 162
Chapter 21 / 1975 169

Acknowledgments

The author gratefully acknowledges the assistance, encouragement and cooperation of the following people:

At CHUM Ltd: Roger Ashby, Warren Cosford and especially J. Robert Wood
At Methuen: Jim Chalmers, Fred Wardle, Steve Eby

And to John Kosh for his perceptive jacket concept
Michael Van Elsen for his sympathetic design
Marnie Collins for her editing

Photography
Color pix, other than those duly credited by photographer's name, were supplied by the following record companies, to whom the author is deeply indebted: — ABC (Bob Gibson); Atlantic U.S. (Bob Rolontz): Capricorn (Mike Hyland); Columbia U.S. (Gary Williams); Electra/Asylum (Karin Berg); Island U.K. (Brian Blevins); RSO U.K. (Helen Walters); and WB U.S. (Veronica Brice).

Black and white pix, other than those credited, were supplied with the co-operation of the following record companies: — ABC Records, A & M Canada, Atlantic U.S., Capitol/EMI U.S. and Canada, Capricorn, Columbia Canada, London Canada, MCA Canada, Motown U.S. and Canada, RCA Canada and WB U.S.

The author also wishes to thank the many fine people who contributed compassion and advice, including Andy Gray, Walt Grealis, John Kosh, Martin Melhuish, Drew Metcalf, Claude Nobs, Juan Rodriquez, Dave Sheehy, Peter Steinmetz, and Lee Zhito.

Other books by Ritchie Yorke
Axes, Chops & Hot Licks (1971)
Into the Music: The Van Morrison Biography (1975)
The Led Zeppelin Biography (1975)

Superior sound provided by Empire turntables and speakers, Koss headphones, BASF and TEAC cassette playback equipment, and Ampex cassettes.

*For Christine
who plucked the words
right out of my heart*

"There is always something new out of Africa."
(Pliny the Elder, 23-79 AD)

"It's got a back beat, you can't lose it."
(Chuck Berry, 1957)

"Let's face it: rock and roll is bigger than all of us."
(Alan Freed, 1958)

"The trouble is that so much of the record business is being run by people who don't have a clue what it's about."
(Paul McCartney, 1967)

"It just breaks my heart sometimes that we're all singing songs about love and peace and togetherness, and really there is so little of it."
(Robert Plant, 1974)

THE DEVELOPMENT OF POPULAR MUSIC

1877	Thomas Edison first records sound; invention labeled "phonograph"
1887	U.S. record industry launched
1891	Introduction of records on flat discs by Emile Berliner in Montreal
1892	Music's first million-seller: *After the Ball* by J. Aldrich Libbey
1893	Visiting Czech classical composer, Antonin Dvorak, tells America, " . . . the future music of this country must be founded on . . . the Negro melodies."
1890s	The era of ragtime or "coon music"
1912	The first golden age of records begins
1920s	Tin Pan Alley comes of age
1922	Rise of radio causes decline in record popularity
1930s	Radio turns to record companies for a supply of programmable music; the Swing era
1941	Les Paul builds the first electric guitar
1948	Introduction of 12-inch LPs and 45 rpm singles; the term "rock 'n' roll" first appears on record
1950s	Rise of independent record companies producing "race music" and "hillbilly" music normally ignored by major companies
1953	Bill Haley's *Crazy Man Crazy* becomes first rock single on *Billboard* charts
1958	Introduction of stereo albums
1964	British rock invasion of America, spearheaded by the Beatles
1966	Introduction of tape cartridge and cassette
1967	Record sales in U.S. exceed one billion dollars
1970	Canada joins Britain as a regular producer of hit records for America
1974	Rock celebrates the end of its second decade

INTRODUCTION

The roots of rock 'n' roll can be traced back into the 19th century to the blues and gospel music of plantation laborers brought to America against their will to be sold as slaves. Music has always been a strong cultural activity of all societies; there is evidence that the Egyptians were holding music festivals 5000 years ago. But it wasn't until the latter part of the 19th century that an invention came along that was to totally revolutionize the performance and exposure of music — the gramophone record.

The humble beginnings of today's massive record industry date back to 1891, when a German immigrant named Emile Berliner produced the first phonograph records on flat discs. Fourteen years earlier, in 1877, Thomas Edison had first reproduced sound using tin-foil cylinders, an invention he called the phonograph, based on the Greek words meaning "writing sound".

Most 19th century American families shared a fondness for music. Some preferred serious European classical music; others liked a lighter, frothier style of popular entertainment. From 1840 right up until the middle of this century, "nigger" minstrel shows were enormously popular all over America, and their fame spread to Europe, where Queen Victoria attended a touring performance. Even a hundred years ago, the black American was exercising keen influence on North American popular music taste.

This fascination of white folk for black-oriented entertainment has long been an amazing paradox. While the majority of 19th-century white Americans regarded the black face as inferior, there was no objection to supporting the development of black culture through entertainment.

1892 brought music's first million-seller, *After the Ball,* and was the year in which Coca-Cola, a beverage based on an extract of the same coca plant that would freeze so many rock nostrils in the '70s, ceased advertising itself as a patent medicine and became a soft drink. "The pause that refreshes," they called it, and it was a titilating idea in those narrow corridors of Victorianism; the public was being encouraged to drink something for the sheer pleasure of it, and to hell with medicinal value. It was the beginnings of fun and grooviness and all that weird jazz.

The course of popular music was greatly affected — although few people realized it at the time — by another, much later invention. In 1941, at age 13, a kid named Les Paul tore the back out of his Sears acoustic guitar and built what became the first electric guitar. But even bigger changes were hanging on the horizon. For one thing, record speeds were changing. In 1948 Columbia Records introduced the $33^{1}/_{3}$ rpm long-playing album, while RCA countered with the 7-inch 45 rpm single. Previously all records had been heavy, fragile 78 rpm shellac discs. Both the $33^{1}/_{3}$ album and the 45 single represented vast improvements.

The same year a new phrase entered the musical language — "rock 'n' roll". A black slang term for love-making, it was utilized in several so-called race records in '48, among them Roy Brown's *Good Rockin' Tonight* and the Ravens' *Rock All Night Long*. Three years later, Gunter Lee Carr recorded a dance tune, *We're Gonna Rock,* which somewhat reduced the sexual implication of the phrase. These "race" records were restricted in exposure to the black market. Very few white ears heard them. But they were forerunners of what was looming on the "hip" horizon.

Millions of war babies were by now reaching their teen-age years. Conceived at the end of World War II in a joyful seething mass as returning soldiers fell into the arms of their sweethearts, we were the product of an era in which contraception was still frowned upon. Now we were flowering in the millions, a field of blazing poppies growing up in the shadow of mankind's single most horrific weapon, the atomic bomb. As we stumbled into our teens, we were restless and rebellious. Freed by post-war economic affluence from the usual hassles of having no bread, we began to express ourselves as no other adolescent generation in history had done. No longer would children be seen but not heard.

Bored by the tripe and triviality that dominated network radio, we twiddled our radio dials and discovered exciting and unique sounds on black "race" stations. Our response to this raw, dynamic music was so strong that it triggered the interest of 2 white men who would play key roles in the evolution of rock 'n' roll. They were Cleveland deejay Alan Freed and a country-style singer from Chester, Pennsylvania, named Bill Haley. With the back-up group he'd named the Comets in '52, Haley had recorded several singles utilizing the Negro slang word "rock". One of their first singles was entitled *We're Going to Rock This Joint Tonight*. In '53, Bill Haley and the Comets landed their first hit and the disc that is credited with being the first-ever rock 'n' roll record to make the *Billboard* best-selling charts: *Crazy Man Crazy*.

In its original form, race music had not been acceptable to the traditional music industry or to white broadcasters. In effect, Haley had taken basic rhythm and blues race music, played it as a white man, and called the result "rock 'n' roll". Haley came back in the summer of '54 with his white version of a Rhythm and Blues hit by Joe Turner, *Shake, Rattle and Roll*. Turner scored a big hit in the black market, but Haley toned down the lyrics to suit the supposedly less-passionate tastes of white folk.

For us, growing up in the early '50s, the main cultural influences were actors Marlon Brando and James Dean. Brando and Dean were sullen stars of highly successful teen rebellion movies, *The Wild One* and *Rebel Without a Cause*, reflecting the link between '50s youth and rebellion.

Marlon Brando would go on to much more celebrated acting achievements, while James Dean —the subject of a growing cult phenomenon in the '70s—was destined to die violently within months in a car accident. The archetypal rebel, James Dean was a victim of the excesses of the Hollywood life-style and his own obsession with outrunning the system.

A song called *Work with Me Annie* by Hank Ballard and the Midnighters was a black market million-seller in '54. It was a straight-ahead, no-holds-barred romp into the revelries of love-making, with lyrics that would turn a parson pink. Realizing the tune's commerciality, but doubtful about such gutsy lyrics as "Work with me Annie, Let's git it while the gittin' is good," a rising female blues singer named Etta James recorded a toned-down version entitled *Wallflower*. The opening lyrics were, "Roll with me Henry, You better roll it while the rollin' is on."

But still the majority of big-city broadcasters didn't consider the song tame enough for mass audience tastes. So a singer named Georgia Gibbs whitewashed the Etta James whitewash, and now the chorus went, "Dance with me Henry, Let's dance while the music rolls on." The Gibbs version was the biggest hit, simply because it was the only version of *Work with Me Annie* allowed onto AM pop airwaves.

Already the forces of repression were trying to stamp out rock 'n' roll. Rock was simply too raucous and rebellious for the battered eardrums of the establishment. No longer was the *song* the whole thing. Now the *performance* was what really mattered in making a hit. It all had to do with *feeling* — some records had it, some didn't.

Clearly some heavy changes hung in the air as we cruised to drive-ins to take in *Rebel Without a Cause* and to come on to our steadies. A broadcast executive named Todd Storz had launched the first Top 40 format on radio WTIX in New Orleans in '53, and the format was catching on fast. The rock era had begun.

1955

1955—a peak year for a generation restless and sometimes reckless for change. In America the war against communism raged on relentlessly, especially in Hollywood, where the motion-picture industry had bowed to Washington pressure and purged its ranks of those who would dare to question the inherent justice and goodness of the American way. Hollywood had no time for the teen market. Nor was the TV tube geared to the interests of the emerging generation. It was little wonder that rock 'n' roll music — often created by as well as for teenagers—would prove to be such a dynamic force.

The number-one record of January 1955 was *Hearts of Stone* by Otis Williams and the Charms. As the story went, the president of the independent King Records in Cincinnati auditioned a bunch of black kids playing softball in a parking lot across from his office. The rest, as they say, was history. *Hearts of Stone* would set the pace for '55, when rock 'n' roll really began to dominate popular music.

Not that rock was welcomed with open arms by either our parents or the music industry. Adults found rock 'n' roll obscene, obnoxious, and intolerable. The established music companies had invested their energies in the conveyor-belt escapism of schmaltzy MOR, or middle-of-the-road music, performed by innocuous and wholesome Caucasians. Rock 'n' roll was a monstrous threat to this snug little status quo, but rather than jump in and capitalize on it, the big record companies chose to ignore it.

The result was that a rush of small independent labels dominated the '55 hit scene. *Hearts of Stone* is an excellent example of their product; the Penguins' super-smooth rendition of *Earth Angel* is another. The song was written by the lead Penguin, a gentleman named Jesse Belvin; the name of the group was inspired by the Willie the Kool character on the Kools cigarette package.

R & B records only became mass-market hits against the toughest of odds. Very few non-black radio stations would program pure rhythm and blues records, considering them damaging, or at least distasteful, to whites. Certainly R & B sizzled with a sexuality totally unknown in MOR pop circles.

The small independent labels gamely defied the status quo and allowed the public to hear a new kind of music. One of them was Atlantic Records in New York, formed 8 years earlier. Their first big solo success came with Lavern Baker, a former singer in a Baptist church choir; her first single for Atlantic, *Tweedle Dee,* was hijacked by Georgia Gibbs.

Other solo artists gaining mass attention included Roy Hamilton, Dinah Washington, Hank Ballard, Ray Charles, Ruth Brown, Little Walter, Joe Turner, Etta James, Little Willie John, and a young man from Mississippi named Ellas McDaniels. Again it was shrewd talent spotting by an independent label that brought Ellas—through his stage name, Bo Diddley—to world prominence. Early in '55 he auditioned for the Chess Brothers, Leonard and Phil, with an original tune called *Uncle John.* The brothers suggested a name change for the song, and Bo Diddley laid down funk unlimited and an all-time rock classic, *Bo Diddley.*

From New Orleans came Antoine Domino with an early one of his many million-sellers, *Ain't That a Shame.* His was another rags-to-riches story. After working on an ice truck and in a bedspring factory, Antoine set about making music. He signed with Imperial Records in

Early faces and phases of rock 'n' roll...
(Above) pioneering blues stylist, Bessie Smith
(Left) the sensational showman, Little Richard, was discovered in Macon, Georgia. While washing dishes at the Macon bus station (below) he penned the rock classic, *Tutti Frutti*.
(credit: Yorke)
(Right) The most significant musical figure of rock's first decade, the inimitable Chuck Berry

While parents mooned and spooned to Andy Williams, we grooved to the raw, raunchy rhythm and blues of Bo Diddley (right), Ray Charles (bottom left) and Etta James.

'49, and his first single, *The Fat Man*, gave him the nickname of "Fats". Although it had turned gold by '53, it took him 6 years and 25 R & B records before his name finally reached white America through *Ain't That a Shame*. Even then he had to endure the competition of a mediocre hijacked cover version by Pat Boone.

Because R & B records were largely banned from commerical radio due to their alleged "obscenity", song pirating or hijacking became common practice in the music industry. Artists such as Pat Boone, the Crewcuts, the Diamonds, and Georgia Gibbs subjected earthy R & B songs to a phony filtering process. As a result, black artists couldn't get air play. There were only 700 R & B disc jockeys, compared to 10,000 MOR deejays.

Yet some emerging R & B artists were so unique that their music couldn't be laundered. The blind pianist and blues singer, Ray Charles, for instance, was obviously in a class of his own, but it took a while for many to realize it. Like Fats Domino, Ray Charles began recording in '49, but it took a total of 23 singles before he finally hit the pop chart big-time with *I've Got a Woman*. This Ray Charles original demonstrated why young people, black and white, found immediate identification with rhythm and blues. It was the nitty-gritty, the real thing, *making-out music*!

The more they put down rock 'n' roll, the more we were engrossed by it. The generation gap was growing. Teen-agers were developing their own peer-group mirror culture, rejecting the tastes of the parents.

The first '50s black group to make it with adults in the pop scene was the prolific Platters, who gained air play on many white radio stations. The group had formed in '53 in Los Angeles with Tony Williams as lead singer and had been signed to a management contract by Buck Ram, who also managed the Penguins. After 11 successive singles for King Records in Cincinnati failed to hit paydirt, Ram moved the Platters to Mercury, where the Penguins were stabled. The Buck Ram song, *Only You*, was the first of many million-sellers for the Platters.

Texas was the setting for rock 'n' roll's first tragedy. On Christmas Eve, 1954, a Memphis piano player turned singer was in Houston on a Texas promotional trip. While sitting around waiting to begin his scheduled performance at the city auditorium, Johnny Ace, playing Russion roulette with a loaded revolver, accidentally blew his brains out. On January 12, 1955, his record company released a posthumous single; *Pledging My Love* was destined to be Johnny Ace's biggest hit and one of the top records of the year.

To many people, rock 'n' roll didn't really begin until Bill Haley came along in the movie, *Blackboard Jungle,* belting out *Rock Around the Clock*. A former yodeller fronting a country and western band, Bill Haley was clearly in the right place at the right time. He recorded *Rock Around the Clock* in April of 1954. Then *Blackboard Jungle* was released and, a year after the record's release, *Rock Around the Clock* started to move. It was a phenomenal 20-million-seller — the first international rock 'n' roll smash.

Almost all of early rock music was heavily influenced by the South. It had its roots in the black experience—the simple, lively rhythms of Africa coupled with the sorrow and bitterness of slavery. The music's message of alienation struck a chord in teen-agers facing the Bomb, the cold war, and a hopelessly unjust society.

Louis Jordan was a lesser-known key figure of the era. He didn't have a record released in '55, but he had enormous influence on several of the year's hottest new rock 'n' roll artists. Bo Diddley once said, "I always wanted to be like Louis Jordan. I dug his style." He also influenced B. B. King and Bill Haley, but, more significantly, his music inspired the most influential of all musicians of the '50s and '60s, Chuck Berry. A strange man with an incredible gift for capturing the authentic feelings of the era, Chuck combined that unique intuition with the free-flowing rhythms of traditional blues music in one dynamic package. He was the catalyst in prodding the evolution of R & B music into the mass-market rock 'n' roll mainstream. His contributions were enormous.

During a vacation in Chicago in early '55, Chuck met blues singer Muddy Waters, who in turn introduced him to the Chess brothers. Chuck had written a tune he wanted to record called *Ida Red*. Re-named, it became his first smash hit, *Maybelline*.

OTHER NOTABLE RECORDS — '55
SPEEDO—Cadillacs
MY BABE—Little Walter

1956

In 1956, a former truck driver from Memphis, Elvis Aaron Presley, was launched internationally by an ex-carnival hustler called Col. Tom Parker
Among Presley's early hits was a rock 'n' roll remake of Big Mama Thornton's R & B success *Hound Dog* (over left)
Fats Domino (over right) would prove one of the most dynamic and durable of rock's early stars

1956 — a great golden vintage year in the hit story of rock 'n' roll. Although black artists had made extraordinary gains through R & B and rock 'n' roll music, there was no such thing as a black film or TV star. Black people weren't used in TV commercials. Black was definitely not yet beautiful. But '56 was the year that would see the arrival of a white Tennessee youth who would become the most controversial and most popular entertainer of all time. Elvis Presley's key contribution to rock 'n' roll was that he, a white, knew *how* to sing black music. Able to secure network TV exposure denied to black entertainers, Presley was the first of many white artists who would earn fortunes by sounding black.

Chuck Berry, the pride of St. Louis, had 3 big hit singles in '56; *No Money Down;* the doubleheader, *Too Much Monkey Business* coupled with *Brown-Eyed Handsome Man;* and *Roll Over Beethoven,* one of the earliest anthems of alienated adolescence.

But if Chuck Berry was the definitive rock 'n' roll poet and lyricist of the '50s, the era's most sensational stage act was Richard Penniman, celebrated around the globe as Little Richard. His sense of showmanship, his buzz on the bizarre, and his elaborate and exciting stage presentation was unrivalled then or now. Little Richard simply knew how and when to get the people off. At the tender age of 7, Richard had sung for nickels and dimes on street corners in Macon, Georgia, but it wasn't till 1955, while working as a dishwasher in Macon's bus depot, that Richard composed the tune that would bring him instant fame. *Tutti Frutti,* like several other Little Richard singles, would become an all-time rock standard.

Another hit, *Long Tall Sally,* was about a girl from Richard's past; later the Beatles and dozens of others would record the song. In the summer of '56, Little Richard came through with his best-known song, *Rip It Up,* which would be recorded by a lot of heavy names, from Presley to Buddy Holly to the Everly Brothers, but never with quite the spine-tingling potency of Little Richard's inimitable original. Unfortunately, Little Richard's fierce emotionalism, his energetic delivery, his whole manner was a little too freaky for conservative tastes. He was too much of the real thing!

Rock 'n' roll music was by now arising from all sorts of unlikely places. One such town was Memphis, Tennessee, where Carl Perkins and *Blue Suede Shoes* caught the ear of the nation with a warning to the establishment. In the mid-'50s Memphis hit the musical map in a big way with an abundance of night-clubs, a sympathetic atmosphere, and most important, a highly perceptive man named Sam Phillips who owned a label called Sun Records.

Sun was founded by Phillips in 1950. At first he concentrated on recording black artists such as Rufus Thomas, Little Junior Parker, James Cotton, and Little Milton. In 1955, flooded with young white singers and musicians desperate to get into a recording studio, Phillips became a central figure in the development of the rockabilly sound. Rockabilly, combining the rhythms of R & B with the inflections of country music, led to the first wave of white rock 'n' roll.

One sensational Sun discovery was Roy Orbison, a falsetto-singing, bespectacled musician from Vernon, Texas, who scored his first major hit in '56 with an original tune, *Ooby Dooby*. The recording techniques in the Sun studios were far ahead of their time. The feeling generated within some of these sessions may never have been equaled. History was being made in that little studio in Memphis.

By far the most important Sun signing was Elvis Aaron Presley. While working as a truck driver, Elvis noticed a billboard advertising a recording studio for hire. He decided to stop in

and cut a record of his mother's favorite song, *My Happiness*, as a special present. The studio happened to belong to Sam Phillips, and by sheer chance Sam wasn't far away while Elvis was singing. He signed Presley on the spot.

The first record featuring the voice of Elvis Presley on the Sun label was the definitive rockabilly tune, *That's All Right Mama*. It revealed the extent to which Elvis had been influenced in his youth by authentic southern blues singers such as Arthur Crudup (who wrote *That's All Right Mama*), Arthur Gunter, and Lonnie Johnson. It was a powerhouse debut record and an instant hit in the South. But Sun didn't have extensive distribution contracts in the northern states, and the first Presley single didn't cross the Mason-Dixon line.

In the background, a flamboyant Nashville promoter named Colonel Tom Parker was laying ambitious plans. Convinced that Elvis was dynamite, Parker negotiated with RCA when the Sun contract expired. RCA reissued the Sun singles nationally. There was little response to these first records, but in February 1956 RCA recorded its first *new* single with Elvis, an original tune called *Heartbreak Hotel*. It zoomed to number one—Elvis Presley had at last been well and truly launched.

He next covered an R & B hit by Big Mama Thornton, *Hound Dog*, which, with its flip side, *Don't Be Cruel*, would become one of Presley's all-time biggest sellers. Never had a white singer dared to deal in such body basics and sheer, unadulterated sexuality. Parents were absolutely horrified by Elvis the Pelvis, but the kids were transfixed. Instead of bleating about secret love and friendly persuasion, Elvis got down to where it was really at.

For black artists, '56 didn't bring any big exposure breaks. White radio stations still preferred white-washed cover versions of R & B hits. Copyright law does not protect musical arrangements, so any opportunist could produce a hijacked copy of an R & B hit using an acceptable white voice. To hear the music they wanted, the *real* stuff, kids had to seek out a black station on the dial. Or they put up with the hijacked copies.

But a few R & B records were so great that they couldn't be stopped. Despite being banned by many pop deejays for being obscene, Shirley and Lee — the Sweethearts of the Blues from New Orleans — scored a million-seller and an all-time rock classic with *Let the Good Times Roll*.

Another smash hit from New Orleans was Fats Domino's recording of *Blueberry Hill*. All told, '56 was a bumper year for Fats. A total of 7 Fats singles reached the *Billboard* charts, including 2 other million-sellers—*Blue Monday* and *I'm in Love Again*. Also in '56, the Platters landed their first actual number-one smash, *The Great Pretender*, and a 14-year-old named Frankie Lymon and his group, the Teenagers, rocketed to number one with the classic lovers' lament, *Why Do Fools Fall in Love?*

Only a scant handful of artists who were popular in '56 have maintained a steady, hit-making musical career to this day. Among them are Elvis Presley, blues singer Etta James, and a fiery soul brother named James Brown. Like Little Richard, James Brown was born in Macon, Georgia; in fact, he once shined shoes in front of a radio station he now owns. In 1955 he formed a backing group called the Famous Flames and sent an audition tape to King Records in Cincinnati. The first single, *Please, Please, Please*, was the opening link in a long chain of more than 60 hit records by the man who would come to be known as Soul Brother No. 1.

The battle between rock 'n' roll and the establishment was still raging. Adults were shocked by the suggestiveness of new dance crazes demonstrated on a new rock 'n' roll TV show out of Philadelphia, *Bandstand*. Buffalo deejay Dick Biondi was fired on the air for playing a Presley record. In summing up the events of 1955 *Encyclopedia Britannica* appraised rock music thus: " . . . The rowdy element was represented by *Rock Around the Clock*, theme song of the controversial film, the *Blackboard Jungle*. The rock 'n' roll school in general concentrated on a minimum of melodic line and a maximum of rhythmic noise, deliberately competing with the artistic ideals of the jungle itself."

OTHER NOTABLE RECORDS—'56

BE BOP A LULU—Gene Vincent
JIM DANDY—Lavern Baker
A THOUSAND MILES AWAY—Heartbeats
HEART AND SOUL—Clef-Tones
TONITE TONITE—Mello-Kings
HONKY TONK—Bill Doggett
I'M IN LOVE AGAIN—Fats Domino
HALLELUJAH I LOVE HER SO—Ray Charles

1957

1957 — and despite a storm of condemnation, rock 'n' roll remained the rage. More and more radio stations were switching to the style of Top 40 format radio pioneered by Todd Storz and Gord McClendon. A growing country influence in rock 'n' roll would be reflected by the success of such artists as Jimmie Rodgers, Dale Hawkins, and Bobby Helms. But lyrics were still not a prominent part of our music. The overall feeling, the groove, the vinyl excitement were what mattered.

Elvis Presley maintained a vise-like grip on the reins of the rock 'n' roll scene. Hysteria greeted the very mention of his name and with Presleymania in full cry, teen-age America had taken scant notice of the presidential elections the previous November. Democratic candidate Adlai Stevenson was a moderate liberal opposed to H-bomb testing and anti-Red witch-hunts. President Eisenhower and his ever-resilient running mate, Richard Nixon, carried 41 states in sweeping the electorate with their policy of progress-ever-onward and better-dead-than-Red. Political pundits hailed it as a victory for classic conservatism. To us, it was just another bummer, more craziness in a decade tottering on the brink of insanity.

Like several other fine Presley recordings of this period, the title song for the film, *Jailhouse Rock,* was written by Jerry Leiber and Mike Stoller. Leiber and Stoller, who wrote and produced records for a diverse group of artists, were once described as "the Gilbert and Sullivan of rock 'n' roll". Not content to provide much of Presley's best material, the team signed the first independent production contract with Atlantic Records. Never before had record companies hired producers from outside the staff ranks. It was a milestone in rock music evolution.

The pair's first production featured a group called the Coasters, named after their L.A. location, who provided Atlantic with the biggest hit of its first decade. Their quasi-comedy approach took the rock 'n' roll scene by storm in *Searchin'*.

Through the efforts of non-blacks like Leiber and Stoller, Elvis, and the people behind Memphis rockabilly, many other aspiring singers clamored to climb aboard the rock 'n' roll bandwagon. The simplest method of jumping on board was to style yourself after someone who'd already made it. Thus, Eric Hilliard Nelson was the first of the non-Memphis-based Presley impersonators to achieve national stardom. In 1948, at the age of 9, Ricky Nelson made his show-biz debut on his parents' family radio program, *Ozzie and Harriet.* His success on the subsequent TV show led him in the direction of the platter scene. After cutting several minor hits, Ricky was signed by the independent Imperial label. His second single, *Be Bop Baby,* wasn't Ricky's best record, but it was a hit anyway.

A new style of rock 'n' roll came from the Tex-Mex sound, so named because of the combined Texan and Mexican influences. Jimmy Bowen scored with *I'm Stickin' with You*, while Buddy Knox, from a town called Happy, Texas, wrote and recorded a tune called *Party Doll*.

But the best-known of all the Tex-Mex music-makers was a native of Lubbock, Texas, named Buddy Holly. By nature shy and retiring, during a local appearance by Elvis Presley, Holly leapt up on stage and gave an impromptu performance. Sometime later a recording studio owner, Norman Petty, put Holly together with a studio band that became known as the Crickets, and they hooked a smash number-one hit with the first single to come from the sessions, *That'll*

Elvis scored with *All Shook Up, Teddy Bear,* and *Jailhouse Rock*

(Left) Jimmy Rodgers brought a country feel to the '57 rock scene

(Over) but Chuck Berry captured the era best in *School Days* and *Rock & Roll Music*

Be the Day. The tremendous success of the single prompted the Crickets to take a crack with another original tune, *Oh Boy,* under their own name. It, too, was an immediate hit. With *Oh Boy* still riding high, *Peggy Sue* was promoted as Buddy Holly's first solo record.

Buddy Holly and the Crickets were the pioneers of a new format of rock group instrumentation, using bass, drums, and rhythm and lead guitars, a format that would ultimately lead to the Beatles. Holly was also one of the first white stars to rely almost exclusively on his own original songs. In retrospect his contributions to the booming rock 'n' roll culture were historic.

Meanwhile, Sun Records' owner, Sam Phillips, wasn't content to rest on his laurels or his bulging bank account. The most successful of his second wave of rockabilly singers was Jerry Lee Lewis. Unlike most of his contemporaries, Jerry Lee's musical career had been enthusiastically encouraged by his parents in Louisiana. At one point they mortgaged their house to buy him a $900 piano; later they were unable to meet the payments and lost their home. But their faith was rewarded handsomely when 22-year-old Jerry Lee hit paydirt with *Whole Lotta Shakin',* and followed through with an even bigger hit from the Sun Studios in Memphis, *Great Balls of Fire.*

1957 brought along Chuck Berry's *Rock 'n' Roll Music,* and all around the globe we were yelling, "Just give us more of that rock and roll music!" It was a vintage year for Chuck. *School Days* was another classic example of his commentary on the way things were in '57. Nobody's records were more ideal for dancing, and dancing was almost all that mattered in '57. Dick Clark's daily TV show, *American Bandstand,* introduced more dance crazes than Arthur Murray could shake a stick at — among them the Walk, the Fish, the Slop, the Madison, the Circle, the Chalypso, and the Philadelphia.

Through to the early '60s, hardly a week went by without Fats Domino's name appearing on the *Billboard* charts. It seemed that nobody could match his gift for mixing a little rhythm with a dash of the blues and coming up with such potent musical cocktails. Fats' biggest hit in '57 was the up-tempo rocker, *I'm Walkin'.*

Like Ricky Nelson, Don and Phil Everly were born into show business; their parents were established country music entertainers, and the brothers first trod the stage when Don was 8 and Phil 6. After graduating from high school, they moved to Nashville and soon met the husband-and-wife song-writing team of Felice and Boudleaux Bryant, who wrote the Everlys' first hit, *Bye Bye Love,* and also the controversial follow-up, *Wake Up, Little Susie,* which was banned in Boston because of its lyrics.

1957 brought the first invasion of musical talent from the wide-open spaces of the north country. In the Canadian capital of Ottawa, a 15-year-old lad named Paul Anka penned a song about a girl who had jilted him — *Diana.*

Sam Cooke began his vocal career as a gospel singer in Chicago, later recording as lead singer with a gospel group, the Soul Stirrers. When his record company was reluctant to allow Cooke to record some commercial songs for the rock market, he switched to a new label, aptly named Keen Records, and struck gold with the song written by his brother, *You Send Me.* Sam Cooke would become one of the most important pop-styled R & B vocalists of the '50s and '60s. His unique style was country miles from the first generation of rockabilly acts and imitators. And significantly he wasn't as 'way-out or raucous as most R & B singers.

1957 was a big year for real R & B hits, as the cover-version era drew to a close. And thus 5 air-force guys in Pittsburgh became the Del Vikings, exploding onto the charts with *Come Go with Me,* a song that one of them had written in a mere 5 minutes.

Meanwhile, New Orleans was coming alive to the sounds of an outstanding musician named Huey "Piano" Smith. A piano player for Earl King's band, Huey was spotted by a talent scout from Ace Records, and with his first single, the double-sided rendition of a Huey Smith original, *Rockin' Pneumonia and the Boogie Woogie Flu,* Huey "Piano" Smith and the Clowns caught the chart disease. Yet another gold hit from New Orleans was Larry Williams' *Bony Moronie,* one of the all-time heavies of the R & B dance-disc genre.

OTHER NOTABLE RECORDS — '57
ALL SHOOK UP — Elvis
I SHOT MR LEE — Bobbettes
LITTLE BITTY PRETTY ONE — Thurston Harris
SUSIE Q — Dale Hawkins
SILHOUETTES — Rays
LOVE IS STRANGE — Mickey and Sylvia
JENNY JENNY — Little Richard
OVER THE MOUNTAIN — Johnny and Joe

1958

Rock 'n' roll's first and foremost singing duo Don and Phil Everly barnstormed the charts with *All I Have To Do Is Dream, Bird Dog,* and *Problems*

1958, and rock 'n' roll was in full swing, with a swarm of new artists rocketing up the charts. The year also brought an invention that would literally change the face and focus of the music industry and of broadcasting — the transistor radio. No longer did we have to stay home and fight with parents to tune in rock 'n' roll radio; we could put our music in our pockets and take it wherever we went. And trannies were cheap enough for most of us to get in on the act.

Predictably, Chuck Berry was right in there, laying down the sounds most suited to our new-found musical mobility. 1958 produced a couple of the greatest singles ever from the St. Louis Tiger, including the classic *Johnny B. Goode*, which has frequently been described as Chuck's musical autobiography. Chuck once described music as "food for mood", and his summertime smash of '58 certainly got right down to providing an appropriate background for the passions of adolescence. Everybody sometime had fallen for a *Sweet Little Sixteen*.

Eddy Cochrane's *Summertime Blues* —like *Get a Job* by the Silhouettes—provided comment on the difficulties of surviving without money in the capitalist society. Eddy Cochrane's rising career would be tragically cut short by a fatal auto accident in Britain in 1960, but in the summer of '58 he was zooming. He was one of the few artists of the period sufficiently skilled to play several different instruments on his records.

Like *Summertime Blues*, the Coaster's hit, *Yakety Yak*, was a song about teen-age hassles in dealing with society in general and parents in particular. Another Leiber and Stoller creation, *Yakety Yak* featured the stuttering sax sounds of King Curtis, later to be copied by Nashville's Boots Randolph for his "Yakety Sax" album series.

The late '50s were noteworthy for a certain comic approach, a kind of tongue-in-cheek irony almost non-existent in rock today. Leiber and Stoller were past masters at the art, and their success prompted other artists to take a shot in that direction. An ideal example was Bobby Day. A singing bandleader from Los Angeles who had written *Little Bitty Pretty One* the year before, Bobby flew right up the charts in '58 with a tune about a very groovy high-flyer called *Rockin' Robin*.

Nobody who related to rock 'n' roll in the '50s will ever forget Alan Freed, rock 'n' roll's first spokesman. Starting off in Cleveland with the *Moon Dog Rock 'n' Roll House Party*, Freed had been lured to New York in the fall of '54. Guest shots in rock movies added to his reputation, and his weekly concerts at the Times Square Paramount Theater regularly featured such stars as Chuck Berry. As a profitable diversion, he took his show on the road around America. To many of us, Alan Freed was indeed Mr. Rock 'n' Roll.

His role in the rise of rock 'n' roll cannot be overemphasized. Throughout his meteoric rise in radio, and unlike most white disc jockeys, Alan Freed had been notably sympathetic to black artists. He frowned on white cover versions of R & B hits, and he often went out of his way to push black singers he admired. Eighteen-year-old Anthony Gourdine was one of the fortunate vocalists to have Freed's blessing. Freed came up with the name Little Anthony and the Imperials, and with Freed's support Little Anthony sold a million with his first single, an R & B ballad called *Tears on My Pillow*.

A softer style was coming to rock 'n' roll. To the delight of the ever-conservative music industry, we appeared at last to be buying a softer, more melodic type of record, in addition to

Conway Twitty (upper right) with private plane and a rec. co. promo man, maintained *It's Only Make Believe*
Elvis (below left) had become the most successful male vocalist in music history
Al Kooper (below right) was in his youth a member of the Royal Teens

In the Coasters, independent composers and producers Leiber and Stoller found the ideal vehicle for their hard rock comedy classics such as *Charlie Brown* and *Along Came Jones*

heavy rock 'n' roll and R & B. There were still a lot of MOR hits, too—the result of a determined music industry drive to take federal heat away from the business. Rock 'n' roll had brought so much unfavorable publicity to the record business that the larger multi-media companies tried to clean up the industry image. *Contacts*, the Catholic Youth Center's newspaper, demanded of all God-fearing Catholics, "Smash the records you possess which present a pagan culture and a pagan concept of life. Check beforehand the records which will be played at a house party or a school record dance . . . . Switch your radio dial when you hear a suggestive song. . . . "

Columbia Records' production chief, Mitch Miller, launched into a bitter attack on rock 'n' roll at the first disc jockey convention in Kansas City. Alan Freed retaliated by eliminating all Columbia Records from his radio show. Meanwhile, a second ratio network, Mutual, joined NBC in banning rock 'n' roll records from its turntables. Mutual's music director said the network would not play any records that were "distorted, monotonous, noisy music, and/or suggestive or borderline salacious lyrics." Banning or burning rock records became a trend in AM radio. Yet one of the more perceptive comments came from Mae Axton, a Jacksonville schoolteacher and co-writer of *Heartbreak Hotel*. In dismissing the alleged link between rock 'n' roll and juvenile delinquency, she said, "The music is an outlet for tensions of today's teenagers, not the cause." And she was right on.

The Kingston Trio hit the top with *Tom Dooley*, the ballad of a Civil War veteran hanged for the murder of his unfaithful sweetheart. *Tom Dooley* was to be a forerunner in the folk-music craze that survives to this day. College students who thought themselves too sophisticated for crazy rock 'n' roll quickly caught on to the more restrained flavor of folk. The Kingston Trio, complete with striped Ivy League shirts, banjo, and ukulele, represented an alternative, less frenzied form of pop.

Constance Franconero, an Italian girl from New Jersey, was a former child star and the personification of the American dream of the Girl Next Door. After cutting a bunch of mediocre beat records, Connie Francis finally took her father's advice and recorded a version of the teary-eyed tune from the '20s, *Who's Sorry Now*. It would be the first of many, many hits in the prolific career of the first white girl to really get it on with rock 'n' roll.

From the Philadephia recording studios came Danny and the Juniors with the rock classic, *At the Hop*. As legend had it, the group had originally called the tune *Do the Bop*, but changed the title at the urging of TV deejay Dick Clark. The enormous influence of Dick Clark via *American Bandstand*, obviously contributed to Philly's emerging in the late '50s as the music capital of America. In those days, Philly was like Nashville, San Francisco, Hollywood, and Muscle Shoals rolled into one. Artists flocked to Philly to make records for one of the many independent labels, and then Dick Clark exposed them to the nation. All over North America, we poured home from school to plop down in front of the box to tune in *American Bandstand*. The show had enormous influence on both record sales and the launching of new artists. *American Bandstand* set the trends, dictated the direction of rock 'n' roll, kicked off new dance crazes, but most important, provided us with a mirror of ourselves, a link with our peers.

The establishment was not ready for the shock news of Jerry Lee Lewis's marriage to his 14-year-old cousin, Myra Brown. His new single, *High School Confidential*, was banned by almost all white radio stations in America, and Jerry Lee's career went into a nose-dive. Jerry Lee Lewis was banished from the front rank of rock 'n' roll because of establishment outrage.

Do You Wanna Dance? was an all-time rock classic by the 18-year-old San Francisco R & B singer, Bobby Freeman, a fave rave of the *Bandstand* audience. Dancing was the in thing to do in those days. A prominent choreographer ventured the astute opinion that "these dances are the expression of total, persisting loneliness and separation. They are dances of fear." To us it seemed like we were just grooving on growing up.

By far the most significant new rock musician of the year was a shy young guitar player from Phoenix, Arizona. Using the newly introduced Fender bass and electric tremolo, Duane Eddy coaxed sounds from his guitar in *Rebel Rouser* that brought out the beast in all of us. He was also the first rock/picker to play melody on the bottom strings of his ax, rather than the top strings, creating a totally unique sound that would be termed "twang". In '58 they dubbed Duane Eddy the King of the Twangy Guitar, never realizing that he would be the first in a long line of guitar-playing superstars.

The red-hot Everly Brothers made it 3 smashes in a row with the beautiful ballad, *All I*

Have to Do Is Dream. Their simple 2-part harmonies had never sounded better; their country roots had gained nourishment in rock 'n' roll soil. Later in the summer, Don and Phil were number-one bound again with a new Boudleaux Bryant tune, *Bird Dog,* which owed something to the pioneering production work of Leiber and Stoller. Their fourth consecutive gold single was another strident sock-rock song from the pen of Felice and Boudleaux Bryant, *Problems*.

Don and Phil weren't the only examples of Country and Western influence on '58 rock. A former textile-mill laborer named Don Gibson scored the number-one country hit of the year with *Oh Lonesome Me*. The flip side of Don Gibson's single was another original, *I Can't Stop Loving You*. It would return in '62 via a smash soul rendition by Ray Charles.

Elvis bombed back to the top of the charts with the blues rocker, *Hard-Headed Woman*. But it was in 1958 that Uncle Sam called. Presley fans went into a state of shock at the news of his army induction. It's incredible to realize that less than a decade later, any rock artists who donned a military uniform other than to make fun of it would be written off as a donkey. But in those naive days of spring, 1958, RCA was able to pump Presley's departure for Germany into one of the most highly publicized events in the history of show biz.

As Presley's troop ship plied the oily Atlantic, RCA rushed out the first of several hit songs recorded at marathon sessions a few weeks earlier. At the Colonel's insistence, Elvis had cans full of new material to fill the gap and keep those home fires burning. With hot singles like *Wear My Ring Around Your Neck,* Elvis wasn't about to go into decline, army or no army.

But a very determined effort was being made to try to stamp out rock 'n' roll. They'd bundled Elvis off to Germany to oil rifles and get out of bed 3 hours before breakfast. All sorts of radio stations had publicly denounced rock 'n' roll. The world's biggest record companies tried to ignore it. And despite rock's continuing domination of pop music, American deejays couldn't read the writing on the wall. In *Billboard*'s annual deejay poll, Frank Sinatra was named favorite male vocalist, followed by Perry Como and Nat King Cole. The favorite female vocalist was Doris Day, followed by Patti Page and Peggy Lee. Clearly the majority of deejays were out of tune with both us and the times.

After rejecting the unexciting prospects of a career as a court reporter, 18-year-old Phil Spector wrote and produced *To Know Him Is to Love Him* with 2 high-school classmates calling themselves the Teddy Bears. Influenced by Leiber and Stoller in his early stages, Spector would soon become the first teen-age record industry mogul.

On the news front, Nikita Krushchev was named the new premier of Russia, while in France Charles DeGaulle became the decade's second general to gain a presidency. A new pope was installed in the Vatican, and Ike despatched the U.S. Marines into Lebanon. As the first atomic submarine nosed under the North Pole, America launched its first satellite. Nuclear test ban talks got underway.

1958 also marked the introduction of stereo on records. Although stereo sound had been invented several years earlier, it wasn't until now that a process was perfected to cut a left and right channel into phonograph vinyl.

The young man considered most likely to capture some of Presley's following during the King's absence was Ricky Nelson. *Poor Little Fool* was his first '58 number-one smash, the first of several for the TV singing idol. Nelson and Elvis, incidentally, shared the distinction of being the only 2 major rock stars who never appeared on *American Bandstand* — Presley because of the Colonel's fears of over-exposure, and Ricky Nelson because of his weekly series with Ozzie and Harriet.

Despite the fierce establishment fight to eradicate rock 'n' roll, the music was more popular than ever. In the midst of the battle, deejay Alan Freed uttered 10 words that said more than anything else about where it was really at. Claimed Freed, "Let's face it; rock 'n' roll is bigger than all of us."

OTHER NOTABLE RECORDS — '58
CHANTILLY LACE—Big Bopper
IT'S ONLY MAKE BELIEVE—Conway Twitty
MY TRUE LOVE—Jack Scott
TEQUILA—Champs
A LOVER'S QUESTION—Clyde McPhatter
BOOK OF LOVE—Mono-tones
FOR YOUR PRECIOUS LOVE—Jerry Butler & The Impressions
SPLISH SPLASH—Bobby Darin
WESTERN MOVIES—Olympics
TWILIGHT TIME—Platters
WILLIE AND THE HAND JIVE—Johnny Otis
WHAT AM I LIVING FOR?—Chuck Willis

1959

The Everly Brothers obviously were not one-hit-wonders and proved their staying power with *Take a Message to Mary, Poor Jenny,* and *('Til) I Kissed You*

1959, the final year of the frantic '50s, and rock 'n' roll was going stronger than ever. Freddy Cannon and Bobby Darin were 2 of the most prominent white rock vocalists of the late '50s, but '59 would be a year in which more and more R & B singers crossed over into pop — among them, Lloyd Price. Originally from New Orleans, Lloyd had recorded an R & B classic, *Lawdy Miss Clawdy,* in '52. Military service in Korea had put a spike in his recording career through the mid-'50s, but you can't keep a good man down, and in '59 he made a classic comeback. For starters, he updated a traditional folk/blues tune called *Stagger Lee* which, in a matter of days, rocketed into the number-one position on the charts.

Donna was only the second single ever released by 17-year-old Ritchie Valens, selling a million and launching Valens into the big time. But his success was to be cut tragically short by rock 'n' roll's first multiple tragedy. With *Donna* still high in the charts, Ritchie Valens, along with Buddy Holly and the Big Bopper, was killed in the crash of the chartered plane flying them between gigs. The shock resounded across America and around the world. There would never be replacements for these 3 stars. They had been real originals.

The record industry had evolved into a scene where anything went, where the end justified the means, no matter what. It was becoming the new Hollywood, where talent would be turned into mathematical formulas for maximum mass-audience penetration.

Despite 5 years of staggering sales success, rock 'n' roll was still not accepted by the music establishment. Far from it. Since rock's arrival, the sales of records had almost tripled in the U.S., but some tired execs were still predicting its downfall.

1959 was not to be Elvis Presley's best year. Despite a regular flow of assorted hype from the Colonel, Presley's absence was definitely affecting his record sales. His only number-one record of '59—and his last chart-topper of the '50s—was a sweltering rocker in the grand Elvis the Pelvis tradition. *A Big Hunk of Love* was to be the last really hard-rock single of Presley's career.

Philadelphia, the TV studio base of Dick Clark—the electronic pipeline to millions of teen-age record buyers across North America — was naturally also the home of several highly successful independent labels. Many of their artists fit into a pre-'60s bubblegum category, carefully calculated to turn on America with handsome faces and lean young bodies. Often the music came a very poor second. Nineteen-year-old Frankie Avalon was a typical example. By squeezing his nose between his fingers, he was able to lay down a unique vocal sound that gave him his first hit, *Dee Dee Dinah*. But by far his biggest was a MOR ballad; the meticulously manufactured teen-age dream rode *Venus* right to the top.

Ray Charles, playing the blues piano and wailing his heart out, scored with *What'd I Say,* one of the great classics of rhythm and blues, indeed of rock. By any reckoning, '59 was another monumental year for R & B. One exciting R & B act was Jackie Wilson, who'd been a Golden Gloves boxing champion at age 16. In '53 Jackie had been selected to replace Clyde McPhatter as the lead vocalist for Billy Ward and the Dominoes, a highly rated R & B vocal group.

The New York independent label, Atlantic, was a prime mover in recording male R & B vocal groups, such as the Clovers (left) who scored with *Love Potion No. 9*, and the Drifters (right) who took *There Goes My Baby* to the top.

Key figures in late 50's rock 'n' roll...
(Upper left) Dick Clark, the Philly dee jay and early mover and stayer in the payola sweepstakes
(Upper right) the Coasters swept across the Rockies with a swarm of tongue-in-cheek hits
(Lower left) Bobby Darin, who splished and splashed his way to the top
(Lower right) Brook Benton, deep-voiced MOR blues singer

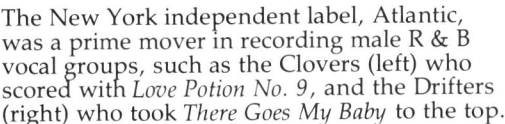

Four years later, back home in Detroit, he teamed up with a song-writing friend named Berry Gordy Jr. to plan a solo career. The following year Gordy would borrow $700 to start up Motown Records, but now he was intent on writing hit songs for Jackie Wilson. The ultimate vehicle for Jackie's soaring vocal range was a smash hit entitled *Lonely Teardrops*.

The Drifters hit gold-disc status with a record produced by Leiber and Stoller, *There Goes My Baby*, one of the first rock discs using strings. Named because of the members' tendency to drift from one vocal group to another, the Drifters scored more than a dozen hits through the '50s with lead singers Clyde McPhatter and Ben E. King. In the summer of '58, the Drifters' manager fired the existing personnel and replaced them with members of another group called the Five Crowns. Leiber and Stoller were assigned to produce the new Drifters and hit number one first time out with *There Goes My Baby*.

An amazing number of '50s R & B groups named themselves after autos and birds, perhaps because both were symbols of freedom. Without doubt one of the most impressive vocal combinations to take their name from the dictionary of ornithology were the Flamingos. Their harmonies were as sleek as satin, flowing like a stream over smooth pebbles. Like the Platters, the Flamingos were not above adding their contemporary touch to an old standard, and in '59 they flew in with their biggest hit, *I Only Have Eyes for You,* which would earn the unofficial title of "the definitive R & B vocal group record of the '50s".

Bill Parsons, alias C & W singer Bobby Bare, offered a spot of social comment on the dilemmas facing would-be rock 'n' roll stars in *The All-American Boy*. It was a song about the great assembly line in the sky, upon which any piece of talent could be prepared for marketing to the teen-agers of America. It was a song about selling things.

The Clovers were an R & B vocal group who'd been signed to Atlantic since 1950. They had a number of R & B market hits through the '50s; then in 1959 they finally found the rock giant they'd been seeking with the Leiber-Stoller song, *Love Potion No. 9*.

Payola, which has been incorrectly labeled as a product of the rock 'n' roll era, was nothing new in the music industry—or any industry, for that matter. Pay-for-play had its start in the vaudeville era, when music publishers provided non-returnable cash advances in return for on-stage song performances. Many major singers, such as Al Jolson, were actually cut in on song-writing royalties. By 1950 the payment of radio and TV disc jockeys in return for exposures was a common music industry practice that continued throughout the decade. What unleashed the wrath of authorities was the discovery in late '59 that TV quiz shows had been regularly fixed to suit the whim of network program producers. TV, which operated upon public airwaves in a virtual monopoly position, was in very hot water.

Having carved a path through TV practices, Congress soon began to sniff around the already tainted rock 'n' roll scene. By November, 3 government agencies were investigating payola practices in the music industry. It was soon discovered that many powerful people in the broadcast biz were using their influence to gain financial interest in the records they programmed. Some deejays operated a straight-out pay-for-play system: Put up your money and you were included in the program; if not, forget it. With exposure, radio license holders had to take decisive action against unscrupulous employees or risk losing their licenses to operate. One of the earliest casualties of the payola scandals was Mr. Rock 'n' Roll himself, Alan Freed.

Through it all, Leiber and Stoller continued to churn out hits. One was a rewrite of a song called *K.C. Blues*, which, as *Kansas City*, would be a gold smash for a singer named Wilbert Harrison. *Kansas City* showed that the laid-back piano sound of boogie blues was not confined to the studios of New Orleans.

The payola investigations revealed that Dick Clark's music publishing company, January Music, was part owner of the Crests' hit, *16 Candles*. Interestingly Clark had only played the song 4 times in 10 weeks before he gained a financial interest in the record; afterward he played it 27 times in less than 13 weeks. When the payola scandal broke, Clark was given an ultimatum by ABC, which aired *American Bandstand*: Sever your financial connections with the music industry or cease your involvement with *Bandstand*. To us rock 'n' roll fans, it seemed that the whole industry was on the take. Rock 'n' roll's respectability—never high—had reached an all-time low. Rock was, in fact, at rock bottom.

Neil Sedaka, meanwhile, wrote a song, *Oh Carol*, about a girl he had known and admired for several years. She was Carol Klein, who would herself gain fame as a song-writer and performer under the name of Carole King. *A Teenager in Love* represented lollipop rock from Dion and the Belmonts, a new group from New York whose name came from Belmont Avenue in the Bronx.

Away from the music scene, Fidel Castro took over Cuba and Russian leader Khrushchev appeared at U.N. headquarters in Manhattan to advocate disarmament of all nations within 4 years. The Boeing 707 jet airliner was introduced into commercial service, cutting the flying time between the old world and the new to 6 hours.

But for rock 'n' roll, the big news was still the payola investigations. To add to the downers, Elvis was still in Germany, Jerry Lee was discredited, Chuck Berry was sent to jail. Yet rock 'n' roll was still there. At the end of the year, Ohio State University announced the results of a survey of musical preferences among kids aged 14 to 18. Eighty-two per cent preferred rock 'n' roll over 17 other types of music. Record sales in the U.S. during 1959 raced to a 20 per cent increase over the previous year. The music business may have been less than perfect—even corrupt—but the music was all we had.

OTHER NOTABLE RECORDS—'59
I NEED YOUR LOVE TONIGHT—Elvis
SMOKE GETS IN YOUR EYES—Platters
PERSONALITY—Lloyd Price
LONELY BOY—Paul Anka
POISON IVY—Coasters
SEA CRUISE—Frankie Ford
SEA OF LOVE—Phil Phillips
SHOUT—Isley Brothers
TEEN BEAT—Sandy Nelson
BABY TALK—Jan and Dean
HAPPY ORGAN—Dave "Baby" Cortez
YOU'RE SO FINE—Falcons
MARY LOU—Ronnie Hawkins
SINCE I DON'T HAVE YOU—Skyliners

1960

1960 — the dawn of the new decade, a period that would bring some of the most frightening, and at the same time enlightening events in the history of mankind.

On the music scene, Elvis came out of the army and, on the advice of Colonel Tom Parker, moved into more MOR-oriented "family" entertainment. His softer records, among them *It's Now or Never* and *Stuck on You*, reflected this new approach, which ultimately would all but destroy Presley's credibility as one of the genuine giants of rock 'n' roll.

And despite the payola scandals, rock 'n' roll reeled on. *Running Bear* by Johnny Preston, the first number-one record of the new decade, was an outstanding example of rock's identification with death songs. In 1960 tragedy tunes would score highly on the charts, perhaps because of the previous year's plane crash that killed Buddy Holly, Ritchie Valens, and the Big Bopper. Ironically, *Running Bear* had been written by the Big Bopper in late 1958, when he was still a Texas deejay known as J.P. Richardson.

Meanwhile, Congress continued its sensational investigation into payola, making headlines from coast to coast. President Eisenhower told investigators to clean up "this whole mess". Charges were laid against 3 record companies—RCA, London, and Cameo Parkway in Philadephia — plus 6 record distributors. Very few key people in the radio and record scenes were left untainted by the scandals.

Billy Bland was a young vocalist from North Carolina who moved north to the Big Apple and secured lasting fame with a rock classic, *Let the Little Girl Dance*. Not that young dancers restricted themselves to up-tempo ravers. There was always room—especially toward the end of an evening when serious pairing was going down — for the let's-cuddle-up-close kind of song. And that was the sort of song that pint-sized Brenda Lee specialized in, tunes like *I'm Sorry*. Rock 'n' roll dancing had never seemed more popular. Just about everybody got into the act. Even the Drifters, one of the most popular R & B vocal groups of the '50s, took a tune called *Save the Last Dance for Me* and turned it into the top-seller of their 14-year career.

The year was also to provide the first rumblings of what would soon become the biggest dance craze since the '20s Charleston. Hank Ballard, the blues singer who would get it started, had been discovered many years earlier by Johnny Otis of *Willie and the Hand Jive* fame. Along with his group, the Midnighters, Hank Ballard chalked up an impressive list of raunchy R & B songs in the early '50s with such titles as *Sexy Ways, Work with Me Annie,* and *Annie Had a Baby*. In '59 he'd written a simple up-tempo R & B tune that would make him a legend and a millionaire. We were still 2 years away from the full blast of the Twist craze, but Hank Ballard would always be remembered as the man who kicked it off.

After a string of hits for Cadence labels, the Everly Brothers made a record company switch to a new operation called Warner Bros. Records. It was a subsidiary of the movie company, a mainly MOR label that had belatedly realized the profit potential of rock. Don and Phil were the first rock singers at Warner Bros., and it was a wise move by Warners — *Cathy's Clown*, the first Everly's single, went straight to number one.

For rock fans the most interesting development in country music was the overdue mass acceptance of Roy Orbison. A spectacled Texan with a taste for rockabilly, Orbison had made a brief venture into the charts of '56 with a Sun single, *Ooby Dooby*. After signing with Monu-

Despite a spell in the Army, Presley's popularity endured through a string of carefully released records and films (left), albeit the movies were proving to be a bit soppy, even for teen tastes
Walk Don't Run, written and recorded by the Ventures (above), encouraged thousands of kids to form neighborhood rock bands
The Everly Brothers (upper right) were lured to the Warner Bros. label at its first rock act
Meanwhile Hamburg's seedy Reeperbahn and its Star Club (below left) was the venue for an unknown Liverpool band called the Beatles
(*credit: Yorke*)
"Little Miss Dynamite" was how Brenda Lee's publicists described their pint-sized prodigy

1960s unforgettable house on the hill, the set of Hitchcock's *Psycho*, fave rave youth film of the era. (*credit: Paramount Pictures Corp.*)

ment Records in Nashville, he wrote and recorded an original tune that would zoom to number one, *Only the Lonely*.

Sam Cooke was another major artist who changed labels from an independent company to where the big bucks were. After signing with RCA, the outstanding blues balladeer drifted in a semi-novelty direction with *Chain Gang*.

The big record companies were by now giving up their bias against rock 'n' roll and signing commercial white artists through whom they hoped to regain control of pop music in the '60s. In the widening climate of integration, it was no secret that they wanted less of that crazy hootin' and hollerin' from the grand R & B tradition, so they invested large sums in promoting the sort of artists they felt should be at the top of the charts — the likes of Bobby Vee, Gene Pitney, Johnny Tillotson, and Roy Orbison.

The '60s also brought about the concept of the singer/song-writer. When white artists found they could no longer find hit material simply by copping R & B songs, they had to look further afield for material. Some of it came from emerging composing teams such as Leiber-Stoller, King-Goffin, Pomus-Schuman, and Mann-Weill. Other singers got into writing their own songs. Johnny Tillotson, a lad from Jacksonville, Florida, was one of the first singer/songwriters. In '60 he had the biggest hit of his career with one of his own tunes, *Poetry in Motion*.

On the news front, '60 was the first year in which America's financial and cultural domination of the so-called free world began to crumble, both at home and abroad. The first big blow to U.S. prestige came when Pilot Francis Gary Powers was shot down during a U-2 high-altitude spying mission over Russian territory. Although subsequently President Eisenhower said the flights had been curtailed, a second U-2 was shot down 2 months later. No longer were the Russians the only baddies.

In 1957, as lead singer of an R & B vocal group called the Gladiolas, Maurice Williams had written and recorded a tune called *Little Darlin'*, which was covered successfuly by the Diamonds. In the new decade perseverance paid off for Maurice Williams. Another of his songs, *Stay*, went straight to the top in the original version by Maurice Williams and the Zodiacs. A new face in the '60s came from Birmingham, Alabama. Jimmy Jones and the tune he co-wrote, *Handy Man*, soon hit the number-one spot.

As the U.S. presidential election moved into high gear, next to Tricky Dick Nixon, John Kennedy came across as a savior of sorts. In accepting the Democratic Party nomination for president, he observed, "The world is changing, the old era is dying: The old ways will not do." "Hear, hear!" we cheered. Kennedy may not have been perfect, or even under 21, but next to the old-line hack politicians he was a breath of fresh, unpolluted air. JFK was a positive.

Even the return of Elvis Presley from a 2-year stint in Ike's army didn't displace the coming election from the newspaper headlines. In the circumstances, Presley did his best, and it was good enough to follow *A Big Hunk of Love* to number one. *Stuck on You,* coupled with *Fame and Fortune,* was the latest in a string of double-header hits for Elvis, the total now reaching 15 consecutive gold singles. Elvis celebrated his return with new recording sessions, another movie, and a potent publicity campaign. But Presley would not regain his hysterical popularity of the '50s. In Colonel Tom's new vision, Elvis was to grow up and become a family entertainer, Mr. Musical America. And what more logical direction than a simple little sing-along Neapolitan love ballad, *It's Now or Never.*

It has been said that nothing shook teen-agers of this period so much as the payola scandals, but the continuing survival and success of Dick Clark proved otherwise. The audience appeared to take no notice of the wholesale manipulation and greed that had run riot in the record industry. As long as the music kept on rockin' and rollin', we didn't seem to give a hoot what happened behind the scenes.

Following on the heels of Bobby Darin, Bobby Rydell tried to go the adult night-club route by changing his style of material. After 6 wild and woolly brass-blasting rockers, Rydell updated the 2-year-old San Remo Song Festival winner, *Volare (Nel Blu Dipinto di Blu)* and landed his fourth gold single.

Hank Ballard had already sown the seeds of the Twist craze in 1960, and he now had 2 more million-sellers to add to his impressive list — *Let's Go, Let's Go, Let's Go,* and the tune that had been the original "A" side of *The Twist*, one of the great, grand-slam rockers of the early '60s, *Finger Poppin' Time.*

On the tube, the 4 debates between Kennedy and Nixon seemed to indicate the way the election was going to go. Kennedy came across as a suave New Wave politician, while Nixon fumbled and bumbled. But the election was a close one. JFK won by a mere 13,000 votes out of 68.8 million.

Walk, Don't Run, a real landmark record of 1960, was created by a 4-piece instrumental group from Tacoma, Washington, who called themselves the Ventures. *Walk, Don't Run* would help to pave the way for the massive local rock band explosion that would dominate the decade. The era of rock 'n' roll groups had dawned.

OTHER NOTABLE RECORDS — '60
YOU GOT WHAT IT TAKES — Marv Johnson
MONEY — Barrett Strong
NEW ORLEANS — Gary "US" Bonds
ALLEY OOP — Hollywood Argyles
TELL LAURA I LOVE HER — Ray Peterson
TEEN ANGEL — Mark Dinning
HE WILL BREAK YOUR HEART — Jerry Butler
CLAP YOUR HANDS — Beaumarks
CHERRY PIE — Skip and Flip
YOU TALK TOO MUCH — Joe Jones
LOVE YOU SO — Ron Holden
OOH POO PAH DOO — Jesse Hill
DREAMIN' — Johnny Burnette

1961

Bobby "Blue" Bland, great R & B stylist who could roar into a microphone and tear your head off. His most memorable hits included I Pity the Fool, Turn On Your Love Light, Stormy Monday Blues, *and* Ain't Nothing You Can Do

1961, and rock 'n' roll was back on the rails, tearing along at a fast and furious rate after the mini creative slowdown of the previous year. Much of the excitement came from a flock of fantastic new artists laying down their first break-through records.

Tossin' and Turnin', the top-selling single record of 1961, got down to where things were really at. It was the one and only big hit for a singer named Bobby Lewis, who had traveled a rugged route to the top. Bobby had sold pots for a traveling Indian, performed in a road show, and worked for the comedian, Soupy Sales. His big break came after the celebrated R & B star Jackie Wilson invited Lewis to New York and took a personal interest in his career.

In the wake of the payola scandals, the radio and record industries were trying their darndest to maintain a low profile, and that meant less of that wild, woolly rock 'n' roll. Yet '61 was a year in which funky music fared better than ever before. There may have been less exposure of hard rock, but we'd gained enough wisdom to seek it out. We simply would not go for adulterated junk — we wanted funk. And there was a long lineup of new artists ready and willing to lay it on us.

Song-writers were fast gaining unprecedented stature in the rock business. Not all singers could write original tunes, and there was a need for a continual turnover of first-class original material, as yet unrecorded. For his first solo disc after leaving the vocal spotlight with the Drifters, singer Ben E. King took a Jerry Leiber and Phil Spector tune about the racial patchwork of New York City and made it an instant classic, taking the trip uptown to *Spanish Harlem*. He followed it up with a Carole King song, *Stand By Me*, later to be revived by John Lennon. The composers of Ben E. King's hits have special significance, as they marked the re-emergence of a rocked-up Tin Pan Alley, a revival of the "song factory" concept. Music publisher Don Kirschner was a prime early mover who reaped a fortune through good timing. Jerry Leiber and Mike Stoller were the true pioneers of a production-line policy that would dominate American-made rock through the '60s.

By '61, Leiber and Stoller's success with the Coasters, Elvis, Wilbert Harrison, and the Drifters kicked off a renaissance in song-writing teams. Interestingly enough, most of the early production work in this area involved white writers working with black artists. A perfect example was the Shirelles' recording of the Gerry Goffin-Carole King classic, *Will You Still Love Me Tomorrow*. Goffin and King were now acknowledged to be the hottest new composing team on the scene.

From Philadephia came the Dovells with lead singer Len Barry and their first record, the chart-topping *Bristol Stomp*, a tune written by the hot Philly team of Kal Mann and Dave Appell. The group had formed in '57 but disbanded a couple of years later because of lack of recognition. Reuniting in '61, they were signed to Cameo-Parkway Records and their career blossomed. In Philadephia, Kal Mann and Dave Appell — with the undoubted assistance of mass

Former Drifters' lead singer, Ben E. King (left), solo'd in the charts with "Stand by Me" and "Spanish Harlem"
R & B continued to dominate teen taste with Bobby Lewis (upper left) who clicked with "Tossin' and Turnin'"; a brilliant girl vocal group the Shirelles (below left); Chicago's Impressions (below right) who featured singers Jerry Butler and Curtis Mayfield; and (upper right) the incomparable Ray Charles

exposure on *American Bandstand* — would become the foremost writers of rock dance records in the early '60s, supplying hits for a variety of acts, including Chubby Checker, Dee Dee Sharp, the Orlons, and the Dovells.

In January, America's coming preoccupation with youth and all things youthful was receiving a boost from no less than the newly elected president, John Kennedy. In his inaugural address, Kennedy stated, "Let the word go forth from this time and place, to friend and foe alike, that the torch has been passed to a new generation of Americans." JFK's shrewd identification with the emerging generation was directly responsible for an upsurge in political idealism among young people.

Back in the Big Apple, singer Neil Sedaka was hitting it big with *Happy Birthday Sweet Sixteen*, while another group for which Sedaka had once sung lead was also happening in a big way. The Tokens took an old folk tune called *Wimoweh*, completely rearranged it and added a falsetto lead, and rocked to number one with *The Lion Sleeps Tonight*.

Despite the outlook of optimism that JFK had whipped up, the global situation rapidly deteriorated during '61. It was one crisis tumbling upon another as the Russians and Americans circled each other like two suspicious animals. Tired of daily illegal emigrations by East Germans into West Berlin, the Russians sealed off the border and began building the infamous Berlin Wall.

In the summer of '61, a number-one record, *Runaway,* introduced a talented Grand Rapids guitar player named Del Shannon. Running away from home had become one of the consequences of the generation gap between parent and teen-ager.

The heaviest break-up of '61 was Dion and the Belmonts. After 8 hits, the group parted ways—and both would be successful. With his fourth solo disc, Dion DeMucci stormed into the number-one spot with a truly magnificent rock 'n' roll record. *Runaround Sue* was written by Dion and his good friend, Ernie Maresca, about the girl that Dion would ultimately marry. Dion performed *Runaround Sue* in the '61 rock movie, *Teenage Millionaire,* which also starred Jimmy Clanton, Mary Johnson, and Chubby Checker.

As if the foreign situation weren't enough to worry about, JFK also had to cope with serious domestic strife. Volunteer freedom marchers tramped the highways of the South to protest bus segregation, clashing with hostile whites in

Out of uniform, Elvis went on a campaign to enlist older audiences thus annoying youth

Alabama and elsewhere. Integration was a noble ideal, but it wasn't going to come easily; prejudice and racial division were still too deeply ingrained in the American system.

America's other priority in '61 was the space race, where the Russians had demonstrated technological superiority. In the spring, Yuri Gagarin, the Soviet cosmonaut, became the first man to reach outer space when he orbited the earth for 108 minutes. America responded a month later by firing astronaut Alan Shepard into a 15-minute sub-orbital flight, and in July Gus Grissom rode the second U.S. mission. But less than 4 weeks later, the Russians came back with a 17-orbit, 25-hour journey in space. It was a war of one-upmanship in the skies.

They might be taking a beating in outer space, but the Americans still had the inner space of rock 'n' roll wrapped up. The toned-down Elvis captured a few teen-age hearts and a lot of older folk with his super-soft revival of the old standard *Are You Lonesome Tonight?*

As a direct result of the dethroning of rock 'n' roll deejays after the payola revelations, there were big changes in programming policy. The jocks no longer selected the music they played. When the payola scandals revealed how many jocks were operating a pay-for-play service, stations decided to appoint music directors to select the music to be aired. The deejays would lose much of their autonomy, but the station management could sleep at night.

Format radio came into being, wherein a short list of most-popular current records was played in tight formation. Deejays were encouraged to talk less and play more music. Format radio brought larger audiences to Top 40 stations, but disc jockeys in general resented the loss of freedom.

Only a handful of artists from '61 would outlast the deejays who played their records. Bobby "Blue" Bland has survived as a cult figure to this day, a sort of singer's singer. Ray Charles, the blind singer and piano player from Florida, falls into much the same category. After a string of funky R & B hits through the '50s, Ray changed labels and went on a country soul kick. In '61 he slipped back into his rockin' gospel roots for the driving up-tempo smash, *Hit the Road Jack*.

On the Top 40 stations still cranking out popular teen-age records, R & B acts continued to dominate. Experimentation in production was becoming more commonplace at R & B sessions, and it was reflected by innovative groups such as the Impressions. After the group's first hit with Jerry Butler as lead singer, Butler went solo and Curtis Mayfield took over as singer/songwriter/producer. His first venture was a trip into a new and exciting direction. With *Gypsy Woman* the Impressions would be recognized as one of the most adventurous vocal groups on rhythm and blues music. Ultimately Curtis Mayfield would emerge as a superstar solo artist of the '70s.

The Brooklyn R & B group, the Jive Five, only ever had one big hit single, *My True Story*, but it was such a remarkable record that they wouldn't be forgotten.

Nowadays singles account for less than 10 per cent of the record industry's total sales, but in 1961 there were only 2 rock albums in the top 50. In '61 all the rock that mattered was to be found on 7-inch platters — discs like the rip-roarin' revival of a 1934 MOR ballad, *Blue Moon*, by the Marcels. Five guys from Pittsburgh who named themselves after the haircut one of them was wearing, the Marcels would not be able to duplicate the success of their unique *Blue Moon*.

1961 would go down in musical history as the year when Berry Gordy Jr. formed Motown Records in Detroit. The Tamla/Motown/Gordy labels would constitute the most successful independent record company in America during the '60s, churning out one masterpiece after another. Berry Gordy had his finger on the pulse of pop music, and in fact he would later admit that a simulated electronic heartbeat was one of the secrets of the Motown sound. Motown's first success came with a song penned by Berry Gordy and William "Smokey" Robinson, a singer and composer whom Bob Dylan would later describe as "the world's greatest living poet". *Shop Around* was to be the first of more than 40 memorable hits for the Miracles.

James "Shep" Sheppard had been the lead singer of the Heartbeats on their '56 gold hit, *A Thousand Miles Away*. In '61 he formed a new group called Shep and the Limelites which, unlike most R & B vocal groups, did not feature any bass voice. They relied on simple 2-part harmony to get their music across. In *Daddy's Home*, they came up with one of '61's best ballads.

OTHER NOTABLE RECORDS — '61

PLEASE MR POSTMAN — Marvelettes
RAIN DROPS — Dee Clark
TAKE GOOD CARE OF MY BABY — Bobby Vee
THE MOUNTAIN'S HIGH — Dick and Dee Dee
I LIKE IT LIKE THAT — Chris Kenner
YA YA — Lee Dorsey
QUARTER TO THREE — Gary "US" Bonds
TURN ON YOUR LOVELIGHT — Bobby Bland
ALL IN MY MIND — Maxine Brown
APACHE — Jorgan Ingmann
THOSE OLDIES BUT GOODIES — Little Caesar and the Romans
BARBARA ANN — Regents
PRETTY LITTLE ANGEL EYES — Curtis Lee
EVERY BEAT OF MY HEART — Gladys Knight and the Pips
MAMA SAID — Shirelles
YOU DON'T KNOW WHAT YOU'VE GOT — Ral Donner
CRYIN' — Roy Orbison
IT'S GONNA WORK OUT FINE — Ike and Tina Turner

1962

From Memphis, Steve Cropper of Booker T. and the MG's was one of rock's first guitar superstars

1962, and it seemed as if nothing else mattered in rock 'n' roll but the Twist. Both Hank Ballard, the song's composer, and Chubby Checker, the dance popularizer, had scored with *The Twist* in August of the year before. The Twist had caught on with us as a dance craze through the winter, but nobody was prepared for the sudden second eruption of *The Twist* in December '61. In a few short months, the dance would sweep the globe, unleashing the most popular dance style since the Charleston, and Chubby Checker would become one of the hottest names in the record scene. Named Chubby Checker by Dick Clark's wife, Ernest Evans had come a long way from being a chicken-plucker in a poultry shop.

It wasn't just us kids who were doing the Twist. First it was the hoofers of high society who let down their hair to wiggle their sacroiliacs, but it soon spread to all but the elderly. The same people who had rubbished rock 'n' roll now considered it good, clean fun. In an obvious follow-up, Chubby Checker came out with *Let's Twist Again.* Established artists like Sam Cooke, U.S. Bonds, and King Curtis were twisting along with newcomers like Joey Dee, who had the house band at the Peppermint Lounge twist club in Manhattan. The Isley Brothers — Ronald, Rudolph and O'Kelly — who'd scored with *Shout* in '59, romped in with an instant classic entitled *Twist and Shout.* But despite it all, the Twist was to be mainly a vehicle for Ernest Evans. Chubby Checker became a world superstar on the strength of his twistin'.

While Mom and Dad twisted around the living room to Chubby Checker, we were up in our rooms getting it on. We were experiencing the first stirrings of the sexual revolution; people were getting into getting it on like never before. The first Playboy Club had opened in 1960, and the magazine was doing incredible business despite widespread religious and establishment condemnation.

A New York daily despatched a reporter to Harvard University to file a profile on a professor named Dr. Timothy Leary. Leary, it was rumored, had begun experiments with a potent psychedelic drug called LSD.

Hey Baby was the one and only million-seller for a singer from Jacksonville, Texas, named Bruce Channel. After 6 months of appearance on the Shreveport radio show, *The Louisiana Hayride,* Channel was signed by Smash Records and hit paydirt first time out with a song he'd co-written with his girl-friend.

Richard Milhous Nixon came out of hiding in '62 to run against Pat Brown for the governorship of California. When the results came in, Nixon had lost by 300,000 votes, which did credit to the state of perception in the Golden State. The morning after election day, Nixon told a gathering of newspeople, "Just think how much you're going to be missing. You won't have Nixon to kick around anymore because this is my last press conference." We should have been so lucky.

The legendary Leiber and Stoller team spent '62 creating more classic records and assisting the launching of their protegé, the 23-year-old ex-member of the Teddy Bears, Phil Spector. Spector had returned to New York from L.A. and was staying with Jerry Leiber while he looked around for things to do in the studio. Enthusiastic believers and boosters of Phil Spector's talents, Leiber and Stoller helped Spector get the gig as producer of Ray Peterson's *Corinne Corinne* and of *Pretty Little Angel Eyes* by Curtis Lee. But Phil wasn't the success in New York that everyone had expected, and he soon moved back to Hollywood to form his own label, Philles Records. He began recording a quartet of black girls from New York called the Crystals, and their third single, *He's a Rebel,* a tune written by Gene Pitney, rocked into the number-one spot.

Just to prove it hadn't been a simple case of luck, Spector went back into the studios with a group he'd put together in L.A., featuring Darlene Love, who'd sung lead on the Crystals' *He's a Rebel.* (It was the only time she'd ever sung with the Crystals.) Spector named his new group Bob B. Soxx and the Blue Jeans and applied a few production tricks to a rockin' revival of *Zip-a-Dee-Doo-Dah,* from the Walt Disney film, *Song of the South.*

Spector was an introverted man who did not enjoy discussing his work with the media. But the entire music industry was talking about his

The 4 Seasons (left) featuring the frantic falsetto of Frankie Valli came from nowhere with a series of smash hits
(above) Little Eva was launched on board the "Locomotion."
(below) The late, great rock sax player, King Curtis
(below bottom) Motown's early hitmaker, Mary Wells

phenomenal records. More than a little envious of the inroads made by this Johnny-come-lately, the king and queen of pseudo-blues songwriting were faced with a challenge. Gerry Goffin and Carole King were asked to write a hit for the ever-popular Drifters. The result was a song laced with heavy social comment and overtones of protest — *Up on the Roof.*

Breaking Up Is Hard to Do was Neil Sedaka's biggest hit of the '60s, a song he'd written with his friend, Howie Greenfield.

On the political front, the superpower games of the previous year continued to dominate the news. The great promise of John Kennedy was beginning to wane in the eyes of young people. JFK was increasingly bogged down in events that prevented him from making a start on the grand new society he had predicted in 1960. To us, it was beginning to seem like that same old weary world with fresh wrapping.

Kennedy's heaviest confrontation was to be with Nikita Khrushchev, the Russian leader, over the deadly issue of Soviet missile bases in Cuba. Although the U.S. had encircled the U.S.S.R with similar missile sites, they could not tolerate the thought of Soviet missiles sitting poised for blast-off so close to the U.S. Kennedy issued an ultimatum, and within a matter of hours, he and Khrushchev took the planet to the brink of nuclear war. Once having outbluffed the Soviets, Kennedy would later make a deal with Castro for the return of prisoners captured by Cuba during the abortive Bay of Pigs invasion in return for $57-million worth of baby food and medicine. A total of 1113 Cuban invaders were sent back to the U.S.

The space race was still burning up billions of dollars as the Russians and Americans struggled to keep on top of each other. The Soviets hoisted two cosmonauts into space simultaneously, while America countered with a triple orbit by astronaut John Glenn.

Dick Clark, ever alert to new sources of corporate revenue now that he'd been forced to divest himself of music production interests in the aftermath of payola, once again came through with a winner. His Caravan of Stars rock 'n' roll road show tore up the highways from coast to coast, drawing large crowds and making another bundle for the *American Bandstand* host.

As summer days grew long and lazy, we looked around for musical escapism, and one of the first things we stumbled into was surfing. It whisked us away to white sandy beaches and thundering waves, the essence of purity and rebirth in a polluted planet. Dennis Wilson, a young surfer and would-be drummer from the L.A. suburb of Hawthorne, persuaded his brother Brian and cousin Mike Love to write a song about the sensation of surfing. The tune was called, not surprisingly, *Surfin'*, and after it became a West Coast hit, the Beach Boys were signed by Capitol, heading out to a million-seller with *Surfin' Safari.*

1962 had barely begun when Motown's Berry Gordy Jr. came through with his latest discovery, a 19-year-old singer from Detroit named Mary Wells. Gordy put Mary together with the song-writing lead singer of the Miracles, Smokey Robinson, and the result was a smash entitled *The One Who Really Loves You.* Smokey came up with a superb follow-up for Mary, the ever-so-gentle rockaballad, *You Beat Me to the Punch.*

Although Motwon continued to enjoy hot popularity on the charts, a new generation of white male vocal groups were making their presence felt in no uncertain manner. The Beach Boys were bubbling up with highly sophisticated harmonies, and they were followed by a vocal quartet destined to be among the most successful American groups of the '60s, the 4 Seasons. Three of the 4 members, including the lead singer Frankie Valli, had been recording since '56 as the Four Lovers. They were joined by ex-Royal Teens member Bob Gaudio, who had written and produced *Short Shorts* and knew his way around the recording console. Playing a bowling alley called the 4 Seasons one night, they were inspired to use that as their group name. Then they connected with a song that would hit number one within 4 weeks of its release. *Sherry* was an "overnight" sensation.

Unlike so many groups who floundered after their first hit, the 4 Seasons followed *Sherry*'s 5 weeks at number one by roaring back to the top a month later with a stunning follow-up, *Big Girls Don't Cry.*

1962 also brought the young singer/songwriter Gene Pitney his first 2 gold singles as a performer, both songs written by Hal David and Burt Bacharach — *Only Love Can Break a Heart* and the title song for an unusual movie, *The Man Who Shot Liberty Valance.*

This was the last year in which Elvis Presley would maintain an unchallenged position as the Prince of Pop. He would continue to cut hit records through the rest of the '60s, but the excitement that marked his pre-GI days was gone. Even *Return to Sender,* the King's finest single of '62, didn't reach number one. It was one of the last great rock records from a king about to abdicate.

Ray Charles stopped rockin' and provided country music with something it had sorely lacked—vocal soul. An old Don Gibson country tune, *I Can't Stop Loving You,* was done up in soulful fashion by the Genius, and its stunning success prompted Charles to follow up with a string of soul-stirred country tunes, including *You Don't Know Me, Born to Lose,* and *You Are My Sunshine.*

The funkiest instrumental of '62 was *Green Onions* by the Memphis band, Brooker T and the MG's, featuring a mean mother named Steve Cropper on lead guitar. It was an outstanding year for instrumentals: Billy Joe and the Checkmates did the *Percolator Twist;* organist Dave "Baby" Cortez rocked on with *Rinky Dink;* and Britain's Tornados celebrated the launching of *Telstar,* the communications satellite.

A Los Angeles trumpet player and former rock song-writer and producer named Herb Alpert was to be the master MOR instrumentalist of the year. He would be the pioneer of an instrumental sound that would sell tens of millions of records and make him a millionaire many times over. *Lonely Bull* was the beginnings of the Tijuana Brass and of A & M Records, both to be notable successes in the ensuing decades.

By far the most significant book of the year was a best-seller titled *Silent Spring* by scientist Rachel Carson. *Silent Spring* contained the first prophetic warnings of the deterioration of the planet. We were appalled to learn just how far the ruin of the planet had proceeded; it was yet another heavy problem to perplex the children of the Bomb.

I Know was a gold hit for another New Orleans talent, Barbara George. 1962 had provided a flock of such memorable R & B records. The Shirelles said *Baby It's You,* the Sensations wee-oohed *Let Me In,* Don and Juan got together on *What's Your Name,* the Marvelettes hipped us to the *Playboy,* and Claudine Clark asked about those *Party Lights.* Rhythm and blues was rocking on.

The rock mainstream began to embrace other forms of music, and instrumentation had begun to diversify. Now we often heard instruments such as violins, tympanis, conga drums, trumpets, harmonicas, cellos, French horns, trombones on rock 'n' roll records. Experimentation was the order of the era.

Few would argue that the strangest hit of '62 came from a Chicago vocalist named Eugene Dixon, also known as Gene Chandler and celebrated internationally as the Duke of Earl. R & B acts of this period were not into heavy dramatic stage presentation, so Gene Chandler freaked us all out when he turned out on stage in a flowing black cape, top hat, and monocle. But his appearance could take nothing away from the unique strength of the song he'd written himself, about himself — *The Duke of Earl.*

Another new face in '62 was Little Eva. After moving to New York from Belhaven, North Carolina, Eva landed a job baby-sitting for Gerry Goffin and Carole King. Gerry and Carole asked Eva to sing a new tune they'd written, and it came off so well they decided to record her with the song, called *The Locomotion.* It became a dance smash.

In Britain heavy things were looming on the hit horizons. In the northern port of Liverpool, 4 aspiring young musicians called the Beatles were embarking on a recording story that would be unprecedented in popular music. An EMI talent scout named George Martin was perceptive enough to sniff out potential in these 4 unruly lads. They went into the studio on September 4, and their first single was released in Britain the following month. You'd never have guessed their potential from the rather mediocre style demonstrated in *Love Me Do.*

OTHER NOTABLE RECORDS — '62

THE WANDERER—Dion
BRING IT ON HOME TO ME—Sam Cooke
DO YOU LOVE ME—Contours
ON BROADWAY—Drifters
THE WAH-WATUSI—Orlons
MASHED POTATO TIME—Dee Dee Sharp
YOU'LL LOSE A GOOD THING—Barbara Lynn
CAN'T HELP FALLING IN LOVE—Elvis
PALISADES PARK—Freddy Cannon
SHE CRIED—Jay and the Americans
DREAM BABY—Roy Orbison
LET'S DANCE—Chris Montez
SHOUT SHOUT—Ernie Maresca
SOMETHING'S GOT A HOLD ON ME—Etta James
YOU BETTER MOVE ON—Arthur Alexander
NEED YOUR LOVIN'—Don Gardner and Dee Dee Ford
I SOLD MY HEART TO THE JUNKMAN—Patti La Belle and the Blue Belles
DON'T PLAY THAT SONG—Ben E. King

1963

At 12 years old, Little Stevie Wonder was the first rock artist to top both singles and album charts simultaneously—thanks to his heavy harp, a dynamic voice and "Fingertips Part 2"

1963 was, by any definition, a heavy year for the new generation, and the most significant and successful year thus far for female vocal groups. Although the Beatles were kicking up a right old fuss in the Olde Country, the mop-tops' leadership of the first British music invasion of North America was still a year distant.

1963 was to be the year of the R & B girl group. The Shirelles had paved the way with a succession of hits, then suddenly the charts were covered with all kinds of girl groups. Most of them produced outstanding music in a new and exciting format—a pleading, persuasive lead vocal over complex back-up parts, supported by a powerhouse rhythm track.

It was also the biggest year yet for the Motown sound, introducing the talents of Martha and the Vandellas, Marvin Gaye, and Little Stevie Wonder. Smokey Robinson and the Miracles found the ideal follow-up to *Shop Around* with a superb ballad, *You've Really Got a Hold on Me*.

From Washington, D.C., Marvin Gaye had been a member of the Moonglows when they scored in the '50s with *Sincerely*, a song co-written by deejay Alan Freed, and *The Ten Commandments of Love*. But the Moonglows were a ballad group, and Marvin felt the itch to groove. He went solo in '62 and was spotted performing at a Detroit club by the ever-alert Berry Gordy Jr. His first record, *Stubborn Kind of Fellow*, was a Top 40 hit. But it was Marvin Gaye's third single for Motown, *Pride and Joy*, that took him into Top 10 territory. He followed that classic with another smash from the productive pens of Holland-Dozier-Holland, *Can I Get a Witness*.

Berry Gordy had another ace up his sleeve in '63 in the shape of a 12-year-old blind child named Steveland Morris Hardaway. Blind since birth, Stevie spent his spare time constantly practicing the harmonica, as well as hanging around at the home of Ronnie White, a member of the Miracles. Recognizing Stevie's musical ability, White took him to meet Gordy. Knocked out, Gordy renamed the lad Little Stevie Wonder, recorded a live performance in Detroit, and released it as an album, *The 12 Year Old Genius*. Both the album and a single therefrom, *Fingertips Part 2*, zoomed to number one. Little Stevie was the first rock artist to ever hold down the number-one position on the singles and albums charts simultaneously.

Surfing was still in. It was something positive to identify with—light-hearted, carefree stuff. The Beach Boys managed to capture the full flavor of the surf music phenomenon when they gave the Chuck Berry tune, *Sweet Little Sixteen*, new surfing lyrics and renamed it *Surfin' U.S.A.*

Sugar Shack, the smash hit for Jimmy Gilmer and the Fireballs wasn't a surf record, but it managed to feature some of the free-wheeling feel of the best surf music. Jimmy Gilmer had studied music for 4 years in Amarillo, Texas, before taking off for Clovis, New Mexico. At the

Motown's unique composer/producer/singer William "Smokey" Robinson (left) was responsible for more hits in the 60s than the Beatles
Other important Motown music-makers included the composing-producing team of Eddie Holland, Lamont Dozier and Brian Holland (above left) hard-hitting girl vocal group, Martha Reeves and the Vandellas (above right) Smokey Robinson's prominent outlet, the Miracles (below left) and the one and only marvellous Marvin Gaye (below right)

Vocal groups, R & B and otherwise, were the big thing in '63
(above left) the Chiffons clicked with "He's So Fine", later to be nicked by George Harrison
(above right) the Blue Belles featuring Patti LaBelle
(below left) California's Beach Boys turned us on to surfing and sunning
(below right) Peter Paul and Mary appealed to folkies
while the Angels (opposite right) looked butchy but belted out "My Boyfriend's Back"

Bobby Vinton (opposite right) tried to keep crooning alive

Norman Petty Studios, where all of the Buddy Holly and the Crickets' hits had been recorded, Gilmer teamed up with an instrumental group called the Fireballs. They'd had several instrumental hits produced by Norman Petty, but the combination of Jimmy Gilmer and the Fireballs was as sweet as candy. And it didn't rot your teeth.

Rock 'n' roll could no longer be classified in one untidy category. The music, like its audience, was growing upwards and outwards. Even the college crowd—which had long since written off rock 'n' roll as being too lowbrow—was unwinding out of beatnik power and black clothes. College kids began to buy records again, and their return was marked by the success of several folk-oriented singles.

Country music had played a role in the evolution of rock 'n' roll, but folk music was coming from another direction. Folk was more concerned with profound statements, with-it words, and too-bad-about-the-backing track. Two folk singers named Joan Baez and Bob Dylan performed protest songs for the first time at the Newport Folk Festival in '63. Peter, Paul and Mary, a trio of folk artists who'd got together in New York's Greenwich Village, were signed by Warner Bros. after a notable gig at the Bitter End club and hit paydirt with several folky songs, including songs by the barely known new writer, Bob Dylan.

As more and more folk-oriented records made the rock charts, the industry did its best to categorize the music. Folk purists deplored the use of electric instruments, while the rock audience considered any music of and for the people to be folk music.

In the southern states, racial injustice was again rearing its ugly head. Despite John Kennedy's frequent pleas for a united black-and-white America, some segments of the population presented considerable resistance. The U.S. legal system pulled the first of many gross blunders that would ultimately lead a large portion of the youth population to lose all respect for American law and order. The non-violent civil rights leader, the Rev. Martin Luther King, was jailed in Birmingham, Alabama, thus giving widespread respectability to a new strategy of disobedience to unjust laws.

One of '63's girl groups had a number-one smash in *He's So Fine* — the Chiffons, 4 foxy young women from the Bronx. The melody of *He's So Fine* would later be "borrowed" by Beatle George Harrison for his chart-topper, *My Sweet Lord.* And while girl groups were galloping up the American charts, another kind of girl had become an overnight sensation. Christine Keeler wasn't in the music scene, but she sang a fascinating tune to the jury investigating the Profumo affair. The British Minister of Defence, John Profumo, admitted having kept company

Alfred Hitchcock again reached youth with *The Birds*

with the young woman in the same boudoir frequented by a representative of the Soviet Union. Profumo resigned.

The U.S. Surgeon General issued a highly controversial report linking tobacco smoking with lung cancer, one of the scourges of contemporary living. The tobacco industry responded to the charges by denying their validity.

Meanwhile, in L.A. the legendary Phil Spector was hot on the case. Spector was a leader in elevating the art of record production to new highs in experimentation and innovation. In Spector's studio there were no rules; nothing *had* to be. All that mattered was the right feeling and a couple of hundred musicians. The current vibe was translated into musical parts; the echo plates were cranked right open; the percussion section cushioned these mini-symphonies of swirling sound with their throbbing female leads. Spector again demonstrated his unique skill by taking 3 female back-up singers from the Joey Dee Twist Revue at the Peppermint Lounge and turning them into overnight stars. Phil named the trio the Ronettes after lead singer Ronnie Bennett; their first hit, *Be My Baby*, was written by Spector with Jeff Barry and Ellie Greenwich. It would be followed by another instant classic, *Baby I Love You*.

Another girl group was the Jaynettes from the Bronx, who arrived with a terrific punch but vanished just as fast. But there were strange times, and few records conveyed the prevailing weirdness quite so hauntingly as *Sally Go Round the Roses,* a unique production that even Phil Spector would have been proud of. (In fact, his brother produced it!)

In southeast Asia, the storm clouds of war were massing over South Vietnam, the beginning of a long and bitter conflict. Already Buddhist protesters were setting fire to themselves in public places, and then came the mysterious overthrow of the Diem regime. American politicans portrayed South Vietnam as a tiny nation about to be engulfed against its will by the evil forces of communism.

The 4 Seasons, featuring Frankie Valli, stomped to the top of the charts with *Walk Like a Man*. Men *were* beginning to walk in a different fashion in '63. The U.S. was experiencing a brief celebration of the new man—moderate masculinity coupled with a degree of gentility. Long imprisoned in gray suits, white shirts, and dull neckties, younger males were adding color to their wardrobes.

The Beatles followed up their debut hit, *Love Me Do,* with a song John Lennon had written as his interpretation of Roy Orbison's style. *Please Please Me* was released on January 12 and hit number one in Britain on February 16, the group's first chart-topper. By now they were bubbling under in Canada, but still meant nothing at all in America.

In London and Hollywood the battle to launch the Beatles was being fought in record company boardrooms. Not even when the Beatles' first album, *Please Please Me*, remained number one for 6 months in the British charts were U.S. record companies impressed. Capitol, the company that had a first option on American rights to the Beatles, didn't even bother to release any of the lads' product in the States in '63. It was a mistake the company would soon regret.

The fascination with falsetto voices was sustained through '63, and provided a springboard for the talents of such new artists as Lugee Sacco from Glen Willard, Pennsylvania. Lugee's first record as Lou Christie, *The Gypsy Cried*, went Top 20. His second record, *Two Faces Have I*, was a runaway smash.

In just under 2 years, John Kennedy had become a respected leader, not only in America, but in every corner of the free world. JFK was up and still rising that fateful November 22 when he and Jackie rode with Texas governor John Connally in a motorcade through the crowd-lined streets of Dallas. Suddenly several shots ripped through the air, smashing into the bodies of President Kennedy and Governor Connally. Commentators choked back tears as they struggled to provide eye-witness accounts of this incredible tragedy. In a very short time the word came through — Kennedy was dead.

Throughout the week that followed we watched the horror story unfold on our TV screens. We saw Lee Harvey Oswald arrested and identified as the lone assassin of the president. And we watched as Jack Ruby walked through a mob of policemen with a gun in his hand to kill Oswald. The nation and the globe were in shock.

A man who would later perform a best-selling song about 3 U.S. assassinations was at the peak of his career in '63. Dion Dimucci accepted a big-money offer from Columbia, marking that label's solo star entry into the rock 'n' roll scene, and had 3 enormous hits — the first a revival of Leiber and Stoller's hit with the Drifters, *Ruby Baby*; the second, his original *Donna the Prima Donna*; and the third a classic slice of blue-eyed soul, *Drip Drop*.

When it came to inspiration, only a few rock composers could compete with Bill "Smokey" Robinson, lead singer of the Miracles. His tunes were as polished as they were prolific — musical gemstones cut with the finest precision and understanding of what love is really about. Not content with merely providing his own group with an enviable and virtually incomparable string of hits, Smokey penned million-sellers for Mary Wells, the Temptations, Marvin Gaye, and others. In '63 Smokey began writing songs incorporating currently popular dance styles into the Miracle's repertoire. His first attempt, *Mickey's Monkey*, brought the Miracles their third million-seller.

OTHER NOTABLE RECORDS — '63

IT'S ALL RIGHT — Impressions
BLOWIN' IN THE WIND — Peter Paul and Mary
MOCKINGBIRD — Inez and Charlie Foxx
BABY WORKOUT — Jackie Wilson
HEAT WAVE — Martha and the Vandellas
EASIER SAID THAN DONE — Essex
IF YOU WANNA BE HAPPY — Jimmy Soul
ANOTHER SATURDAY NIGHT — Sam Cooke
DA DOO RON RON — Crystals
THE MONKEY TIME — Major Lance
SHAKE A TAIL FEATHER — 5 Du-Tones
WALKIN' THE DOG — Rufus Thomas
RHYTHM OF THE RAIN — Cascades
SO MUCH IN LOVE — Tymes
MY BOYFRIEND'S BACK — Angels
YOU CAN'T SIT DOWN — Dovells
CRY BABY — Garnett Mimms and the Enchanters
JUST ONE LOOK — Doris Troy
SURFER GIRL — Beach Boys
PART TIME LOVE — Little Johnnie Taylor
HEY GIRL — Freddie Scott
FOOLISH LITTLE GIRL — Shirelles
IF YOU NEED ME — Solomon Burke
MEMPHIS — Lonnie Mack

Below left:
Frank Sinatra, from the old school of nice-guy crooners predominant in the pre-rock 'n' roll era
Below right:
Ray Charles fused gospel music with the blues to produce a dynamic hunk of funk
Upper right:
The Impressions, a brilliant R & B vocal group featuring Curtis Mayfield

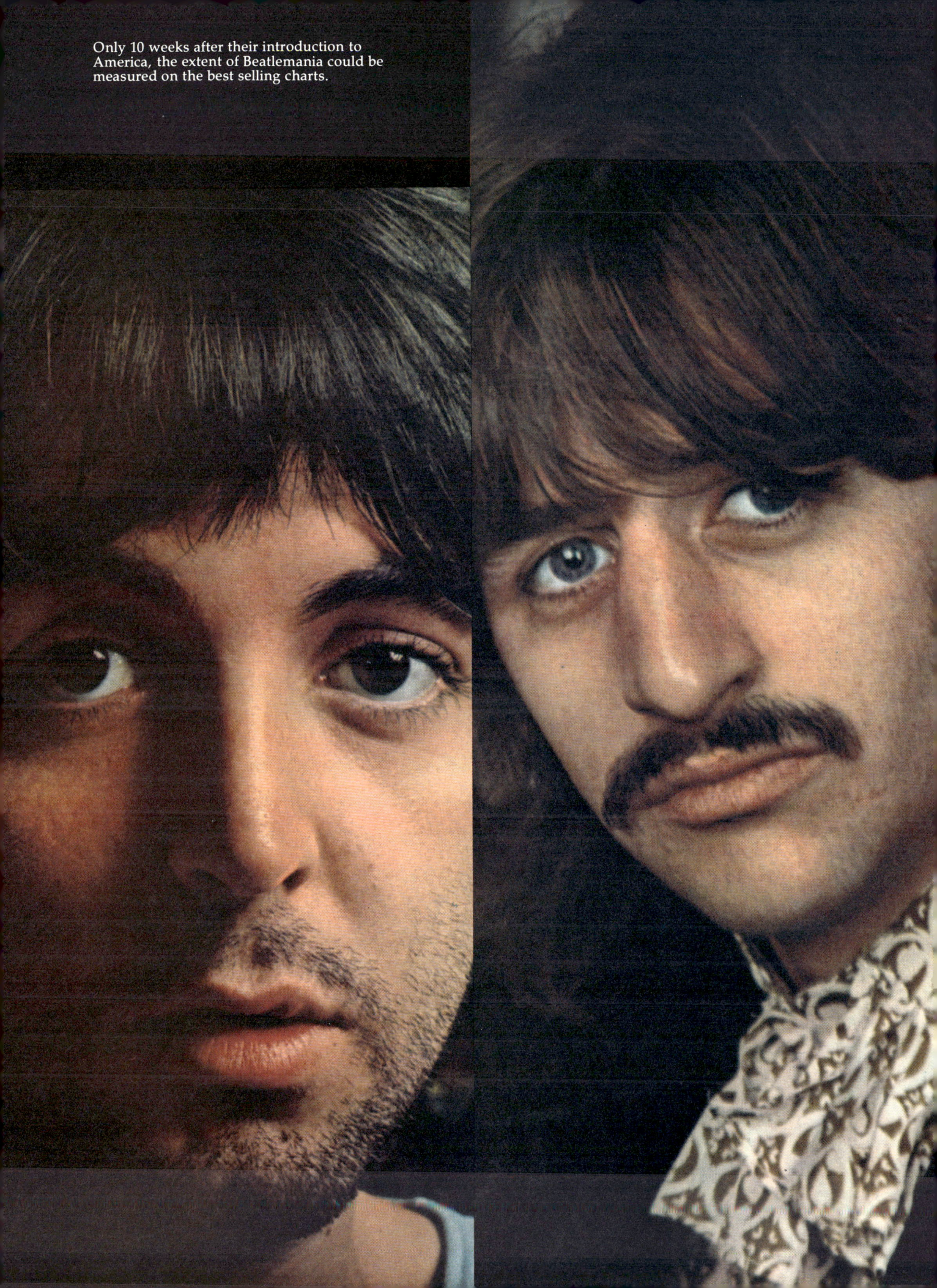

Only 10 weeks after their introduction to America, the extent of Beatlemania could be measured on the best selling charts.

Left:
Solomon Burke, great R & B vocalist tearing up the Apollo audience in Harlem

Below bottom:
Booker T and the MG's, one of rock's early instrumental bands featuring the influential guitarist, Steve Cropper (*credit: Ritchie Yorke*)

Below middle:
The Star Club, humble beginnings for the Beatles on the Reeperbahn in seedy, red-light Hamburg (*credit: Ritchie Yorke*)

Below top:
Bobby Vinton, velvet-voiced balladeer

Opposite:
Dionne Warwick, a gifted R & B singer

Opposite:
The "wicked" Wilson Pickett, gusty and gutsy R & B shouter who scored strongly in the mid-'60s
Below:
Carly Simon, much-mouthed superstar of the '70s, betrothed to James Taylor (*credit: Emerson-Loew*)
Right:
The Beach Boys, among America's most important vocal groups of the '60s

Opposite top left:
Tony Orlando and Dawn, bubblegum wonders of the '70s catering to the weeny teen audience (*credit: Norman Seef*)

Opposite top right:
Van Morrison, among rock's most celebrated singer/song-writers

Opposite bottom:
Herman's Hermits, hot British bubblegum group of the mid-'60s

Right:
Queen, heavy metal kids from the '70s in the Led Zep mold (*credit: Bob Gruen*)

Below:
Paul Revere and the Raiders, manufactured as America's answer to the aura of the British invasion

Opposite:
Jimi Hendrix, guitar player extraordinary and a superb showman — a genuine rock legend

Right:
Cream (left to right, Eric Clapton, Ginger Baker and Jack Bruce) reflected rock's romance with the blues in the late '60s

Below:
The Beatles, cartooned for the superb film, *Yellow Submarine* (credit: King Features-Subafilms Ltd, 1968)

Upper left:
Joni Mitchell, brilliant Canadian-born singer and song-writer

Lower left:
The Bee Gees, the brothers Gibb (left to right, Maurice, Robin and Barry), gifted vocal group of the '60s and '70s

Lower right:
Union Gap set the charts aflame with assorted odes to the beauty of very young ladies

Opposite:
Eric Clapton, described as the "God of the Guitar" in the '60s

Left:
Jesse Colin Young, acclaimed leader of the Youngbloods whose talent remains to be recognized by the mass audience

Upper left:
Linda Ronstadt, among the foremost ladies in mid-'70s rock as produced by Peter Asher of Peter and Gordon fame (credit: Bonnie Lippel)

Upper right:
Pete Townshend, guitarist and composer of the Who, in the doorway of his South London home (credit: Annette Carter)

Below:
A pensive Peter Townshend explains how his historic rock opera, *Tommy*, was created (credit: Annette Carter)

LOWDOWN ON THE ENGLISH POP SCENE
BY RITCHIE YORKE

The late-'60s witnessed a heady awareness explosion in the rock scene, sparked by the acid-era Beatles and their superb *Sgt. Pepper* concept LP. Newly bethrothed John Lennon and Yoko Ono plunged into their War Is Over campaign, offering bed-ins for peace in Amsterdam and Montreal (upper right). It was serious stuff: the Lennons were accorded historic political acknowledgment when they met with Canada's PM Trudeau in December '69 (below). But it wasn't all doves and roses. John Lennon (opposite) contemplates "how hard it can be" at Ronnie Hawkins' Ontario farm in the decade's final days (*credit: Annette Carter*)

Led Zeppelin, the world's most popular rock group of the '70s, soared to the superstar stratosphere with a succession of heavy metal albums and highly persuasive concert performances. The band includes Jimmy Page on lead guitar, drummer John Bonham, bass and keyboards player John Paul Jones, and singer Robert Plant. One of the most charismatic performers in rock history, Robert Plant is seen (left and upper right) striking a characteristic pre-Raphaelite pose. Below the band performs the final concert of its record-breaking '73 tour at Madison Square Garden in New York (*credit: Ritchie Yorke*)

Key figures in early-'70s rock

Opposite upper left:
A short-haired Eric Clapton cutting his first solo album (*credit: Annette Carter*)

Opposite upper right:
James Taylor, among the most successful singer/song-writers

Opposite lower left:
Ronnie Hawkins, infamous rockabilly star, and friend (*credit: Ritchie Yorke*)

Opposite lower right:
Alice Cooper, one of the more bizarre stars of the space age

Right:
Radio London's off-shore studios and transmitter, bringing the Top 40 to rock-starved British teens in the '60s (*credit: Ritchie Yorke*)

Below:
An example of the fruits of rock superstardom—a 17th century Tudor manor house in Elstead, Surrey, sold by actor Peter Sellers to Ringo Starr and then rented to expatriate American, Steve Stills (*credit: Ritchie Yorke*)

Opposite upper left:
Aretha Franklin, best-selling female recording artist in history and truly "Lady Soul"

Opposite upper right:
The Association, West Coast ballad group of the late-'60s

Opposite below:
The Spencer Davis Group, featuring the brilliant singer and musician, Stevie Winwood

Right:
Jimmy Page, leader of Led Zep and rock's reigning guitar superstar (credit: Ritchie Yorke)

Below:
One of rock's romantic couplings, Lulu and then-husband Maurice Gibb at home on Hampstead Hill, London, 1970 (credit: Annette Carter)

Opposite upper left:
America, comically called "A horse with no Neil"

Opposite upper middle:
The Bee Gees in a setting suited to the extent of their success

Opposite upper right:
Rod Stewart, the gravelly-voiced, Sam Cooke-influenced British blues singer

Opposite lower left:
Ry Cooder, distinctive slide guitarist overdue for solo stardom

Opposite lower right:
The Buffalo Springfield with Steve Stills and Neil Young only barely recognizable

Opposite bottom:
Neil Young, cult-hero singer/song-writer of the early-'70s

Upper right:
Seals and Crofts, folkish refugees from the '50s instrumental band the Champs

Lower right:
The Doobies, hot-rocking favorites of the mid-'70s

Below:
The Eagles, currently rock's finest harmony vocal group

The short-lived superstar success of the Monkees demonstrated how the rock audience could be easily manipulated by shrewd merchandizers. The Monkees were the most successful of all manufactured groups, thanks to a TV series, teen mags and ultra-commercial singles. Ultimately the band dissolved under bitter critical fire. Solo talents such as Michael Nesmith (upper left) remain ignored to this day

Upper right:
Late-blossoming vocalist, Eric Clapton on tour in '74

Below:
Bad Company, among the hottest new hard rock bands of the mid 70s

Despite intense competition, England's multi-talented entertainer, Elton John, remains the reigning solo superstar of the '70s rock scene. To rock audiences around the globe, Elton is the catalyst to fancy and fantasy, a trip away from the omnipresent now. His melodies, coupled with the lyrics of Bernie Taupin, are instantly memorable and highly sophisticated. In '74, he signed the largest record deal in music history (guaranteeing him $8 million) and plunged into a spectacular and exhausting North American tour. Elton literally revels in hard work and success and sets high concert PA standards. *(credit: Ritchie Yorke)*

Opposite:
A group of current rock successes

Upper left:
Cher

Upper right:
Gordon Lightfoot

Lower left:
Stevie Winwood, leader of the outstanding British group, Traffic (*credit: Rainbow Photo*)

Lower right:
Cat Stevens

Right:
Canadian singer/song-writer Terry Jacks who landed the top-selling single of '74 with an unlikely combination of a Jacques Brel melody, Rod McKuen lyrics and a song called *Seasons in the Sun*. The single sold in excess of 9 million copies, making it one of rock's all-time ten top singles... and bringing considerable royalties to Terry Jacks, seen here relaxing on his spectacular Pemberton, B.C. ranch, 100 miles north of Vancouver. (*credit: Ritchie Yorke*)

Over:
Gregg Allman of the Allman Brothers Band, America's most successful homegrown group of the '70s (*credit: A. K. Burton*)

1964

'64 saw the launching of the Beatles in North America, a phenomenon unprecedented in rock history. Britain was quick to realize the value of reversing the rock 'n' roll flow and music became a key export.

1964 will always be remembered as the year of the British invasion of American charts. Led by the Beatles, the invasion brought some 2 dozen groups across the Atlantic to tremendous success in America.

The Beatles' third European hit, *She Loves You*, was written by John Lennon and Paul McCartney while on tour. It had been released in August and was an enormous hit in the U.K. Yet on New Year's Day, 1964, Americans still knew nothing about the Beatles. The U.S. was still recovering from the assassination of John Kennedy. Lyndon Johnson had been sworn in as the 36th president, and the country was slowly getting back to business.

EMI, the Beatles' British-based record company, was having trouble convincing its U.S. branch office to release Beatles product in America. Capitol execs in Hollywood insisted that the Beatles' records were not suitable for the American market. The result was that their first 4 singles were released in '63 by various American labels, but they'd made no impression. Clearly, what the Beatles needed was a huge promotion push in the U.S. They got it. A heavy publicity campaign was arranged to tie in with the release of the fifth Beatles single, January 18, and within 2 weeks of its release, *I Want to Hold Your Hand* had made the Beatles the hottest thing in American rock 'n' roll since Elvis Presley.

Only 10 weeks after their introduction to America, the extent of Beatlemania could be measured on the best-selling charts. The Beatles had the top 5 singles, the fifth being the follow-up to *I Want to Hold Your Hand*, Paul McCartney's tune, *Can't Buy Me Love*. In March the ever-irreverent Beatles began work with director Richard Lester on the first film—*A Hard Day's Night*. A single and album were released to tie in with the film, and the single went to number one in its second week on the U.S. charts.

Other British groups followed. *Glad All Over* and *Bits and Pieces* were 2 gold singles for the Dave Clark Five, who for a time looked like they might provide some earnest competition for the Beatles in America. But their fame was short-lived; by late '67 they would fade away. Manfred Mann, a band that had been highly influenced by America's R & B girl vocal groups, revived the Jeff Barry–Ellie Greenwich song, *Doo Wah Diddy Diddy*, and went to the top of the charts.

For a while the American music industry welcomed the newcomers. They brought the kids into the record stores and caused mass-media focus on the music scene. But before long, the major U.S. record companies began to view British rock as a threat to their control of American disc-buying habits. Lacking the perception to capitalize on the British invasion, many major companies were left behind. They now mounted a mass lobby with the American Musicians' Union and soon made it difficult for British groups to gain U.S. working visas.

This unofficial ban caused considerable damage to many British acts, but others were able to get through the hassles. Eric Burdon and the Animals obviously had the right ears in the right places, for they were one of the first British bands to cross the Atlantic. The 4 musicians came from Newcastle, another northern English city, and they were even more attracted to raw black blues than were the Beatles. With Eric Burdon's wrenching vocals and the outstanding

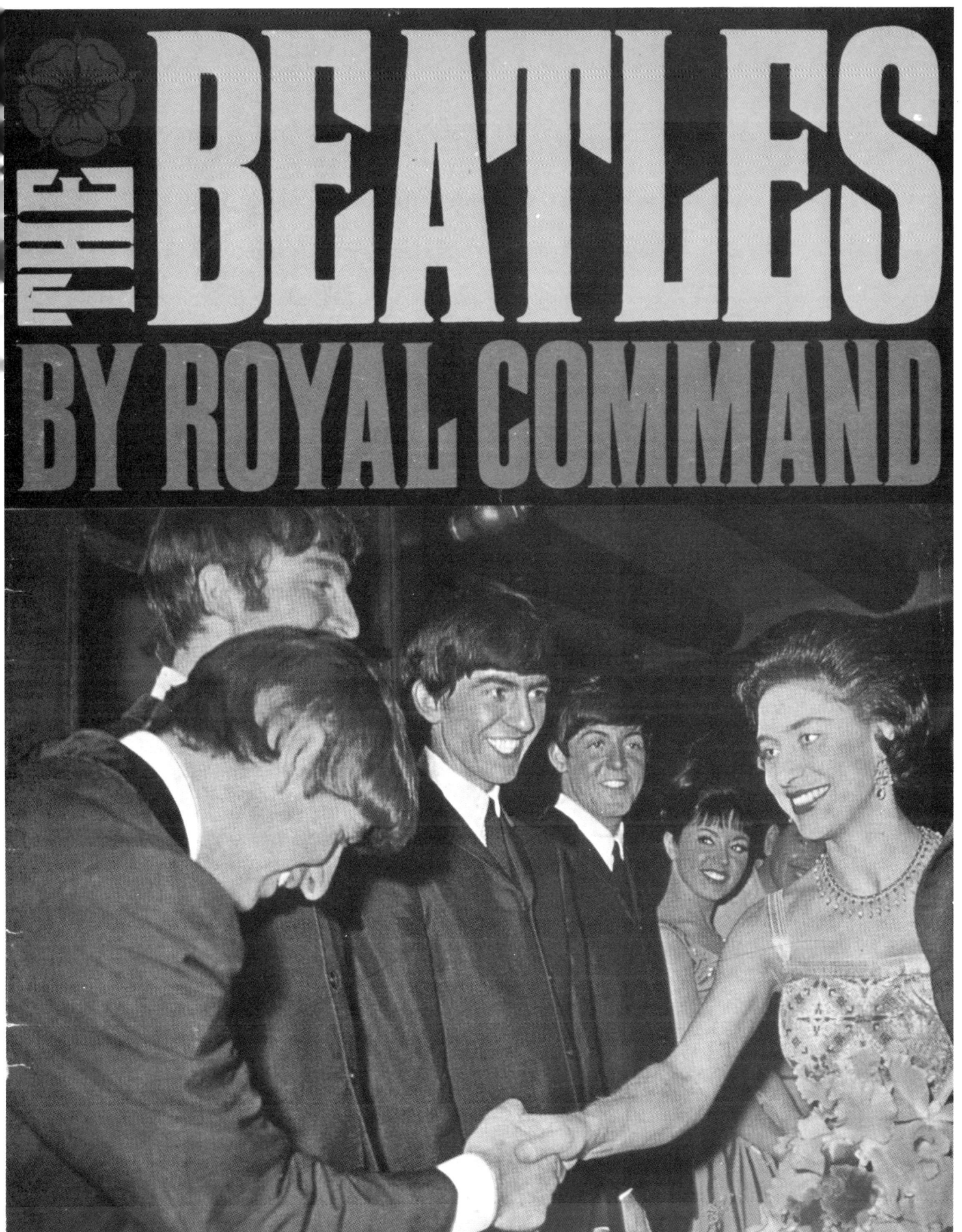

The Beatles paved the way for a flock of British groups to conquer America:
(Opposite left) Manfred Mann
(Opposite right) the Kinks leader, Rae Davies, a budding rock intellectual
(Below left) Eric Burdon and the Animals
(Below right) Mick Jagger, front man extraordinary
(Below) and his chart-winning team the Rolling Stones
(Right) the Dave Clark 5, "Glad All Over" with reason

keyboard playing of Alan Price, the Animals rocked to number one with the reworking of a traditional folk/blues standard, *The House of the Rising Sun.*

The majority of U.K. acts were really only reviving American R & B hits, for the simple reason that most black records had never been hits in Britain during the '50s. Many of the British records may not have been technically brilliant by U.S. standards, but they captured hard-to-define feelings, which outweighed technical deficiencies. Few of the stars of this first year of the invasion would survive, but one was a band called the Kinks. Their music has maintained a cult following with a minority of the audience up to the present. Yet the Kinks never really achieved the superstardom that their music warranted, right back to that first single of the Ray Davies song, *You Really Got Me,* a righteous riff tune.

Taking the resources of rhythm and blues, the British groups then worked on their image, trying to project to as wide an audience as possible. Some very shrewd merchandising minds applied themselves to this aspect of the rock business, and bands such as the Rolling Stones were launched in unique style. The Stones had been discovered playing at the Crawdaddy Club in Richmond, a south London suburb, and they cut their first disc, the Chuck Berry song, *Come On,* in May '63. The Stones pursued a completely different image from the Beatles'; they were intensely anti-establishment, rude, defiant, cynical, and aggressive. If the Beatles enjoyed being the good guys, the Stones were determined to be the bad guys.

The Stones' lead guitarist, Keith Richard, considered the prime musical force in the Stones, literally worshipped Chuck Berry. But while the Stones were letting their Chuck Berry infatuation hang out, the poet laureate of '50s rock 'n' roll was cooling his heels behind bars on a trumped-up morals charge. He had made no records between '60 and early '64, then came back with several outstanding records, including *Nadine, You Never Can Tell,* and *Promised Land.* His biggest single in '64 was the million-selling anthem about the aimlessness of adolescence, *No Particular Place to Go.*

The 4 Seasons had another Bob Crewe–Bob Gaudio smash in *Dawn (Go Away).* It was their first release for the Philips label, and had it not been for the Beatles holding down the top 3 chart slots, *Dawn* would have been an automatic chart-topper.

Even the Beach Boys, hot as a dragster exhaust after a string of hits, found it hard going with their first great single of '64, *Fun Fun Fun.* But with their 4 Freshman-style harmonies, the Beach Boys were so good that they couldn't be ignored. While on tour in Australia, Brian Wilson penned a new tune for the group, destined to become their first number-one record. *I Get Around,* which summed up the Beach Boys' previous musical statements, remained at number one for a whole month before the Beatles returned with *A Hard Day's Night.*

Martha and the Vandellas scored with a classic dance song written by Marvin Gaye and arranger Mickey Stevenson, *Dancing in the Street.* This and other hot soul sounds coming out of the Motor City represented the only U.S. music style to provide a sustained resistance to the British invasion. 1964 also saw the beginning of the go-go era. America's first discotheque, Le Club, had opened in Manhattan in '61, but it wasn't until 3 years later that the short-lived '60s disco craze reached its peak. Dance floors were jammed with people doing the Bird, the Monkey, the Jerk, the Frug, and others. The Twist was dead and buried, merely a memory.

Where Did Our Love Go would be the first of many number-one hits for Motown's pièce de résistance, a girl group appropriately named the Supremes. The sensational song and production were courtesy of Holland-Dozier-Holland. Berry Gordy Jr. had first auditioned the 3 girls—Diana Ross, Mary Wilson, and Florence Ballard—in 1960 when they were known as the Primettes and still in high school. Gordy was impressed but told them to contact him when they'd finished school. Flo Ballard suggested the name change to the Supremes, and the trio were signed by Berry Gordy as background singers in '62. It took several singles till Holland-Dozier-Holland connected with the right direction, and then it seemed as if nothing could stop them, not even the Beatles. Their second big hit was *Baby Love,* featuring the super-seductive vocal of Diana Ross. The Supremes epitomized the vitality and commercial appeal of Motown music — first-class songs given a powerhouse backing track, creamy vocals, and hot mixing. The formula was supremely accurate.

A classic summer record by the ever-popular Drifters, who had 5 chart records in '64, *Under the Boardwalk* would be the group's biggest seller and later the central myth of a collage book called *Rock Dreams.*

A former gospel singer from East Orange, New Jersey, Dionne Warwick went pop with another Hal David–Burt Bacharach classic, *Walk On By.* Under the direction of composer and arranger Bacharach, Ms. Warwick would have many more hits in the '60s.

Continuing crises were the order of the international day. The Chinese, with foreign troops on their doorstep in southeast Asia, tested their first nuclear device. The Soviet Communist Party decided to retire Khrushchev from his position as head of the Soviet Union. And in the U.S. presidential elections, Lyndon B. Johnson and Hubert Humphrey were swept back into the White House in a landslide victory over conservative Republican Barry Goldwater.

The civil-rights controversy remained a tinder-box issue. LBJ tried to implement fair and reasonable laws, but the public didn't appear ready to accept them. In Mississippi, 3 civil rights workers were found murdered. The enormous frustration and bitterness of black people began to manifest itself in a new kind of street violence.

It came as no surprise when Jack Ruby was convicted of murdering Lee Harvey Oswald; the world had been witness to the gruesome shooting of the JFK assassination suspect. Ruby, who had developed cancer, would not live much longer. The Warren Commission released its verdict that Kennedy had been killed by a lone assassin and dismissed all conspiracy theories. But doubts would linger.

The only intelligent media coverage of the rock scene in America was in the newly founded *Los Angeles Free Press,* the first of a wave of alternative culture newspapers. The *Free Press* gave extensive coverage to mass arrests on the Berkeley campus during the predecessors of a series of large-scale demonstrations against the status quo.

One of the most moving songs that Sam Cooke would ever write, *A Change Is Gonna Come,* was to be one of his last. On December 11, at age 29, Sam Cooke was shot to death in a Los Angeles motel by the female owner, who claimed self-defense. His death was the most serious loss since the plane crash that killed Buddy Holly and others in 1959. With 30 hits already to his credit and another 6 set for posthumous release, Sam Cooke left behind an impressive musical monument.

The honor of being the last American rock group to top the U.S. charts prior to the new era of British-dominated music went to an unlikely band from Portland, Oregon, known as the Kingsmen. One evening late in 1962, the Kingsmen's club performance at the Chase Nightspot was recorded live and subsequently released as an album. The set had included a song called *Louie Louie,* written by an obscure R & B singer from L.A. named Richard Berry. Radio station play forced the release of *Louie* as a single, and it literally exploded to number one, becoming an instant rock classic and the center of a censorship controversy. During a congressional investigation into alleged obscenity in rock lyrics, it was claimed that if you played *Louie Louie* at different speeds, you could detect obscene words. Although it wasn't true, we did tend to supply *Louie* with our own suggestive lyrics. It was *that* sort of sleazy song.

OTHER NOTABLE RECORDS — '64
OH PRETTY WOMAN — Roy Orbison
MY GUY — Mary Wells
LEADER OF THE PACK — Shangri-Las
BABY I NEED YOUR LOVING — Four Tops
HI HEEL SNEAKERS — Tommy Tucker
GOIN' OUT OF MY HEAD — Little Anthony & the Imperials
SHE'S NOT THERE — Zombies
LOUIE LOUIE — Kingsmen
CHAPEL OF LOVE — Dixie-Cups
JUST LIKE ROMEO AND JULIET — Reflections
SHOOP SHOOP SONG — Betty Everett
MEMPHIS — Johnny Rivers
RAG DOLL — Four Seasons
OH NO NOT MY BABY — Maxine Brown
RUNNING OUT OF FOOLS — Aretha Franklin
BREAD AND BUTTER — Newbeats

1965

Key creative forces in mid-60s rock—
(Above) the Byrds, a fusion of folk and rock
(Below) the Beatles, unique combination utilizing virtually everything that had gone down before in music

1965, and the Beatles burned on brightly with a succession of number-one hits. And the Rolling Stones' *The Last Time* would be the beginning of one of the most lucrative song-writing partnerships in the next decade of rock.

From early feeble attempts at imitating American R & B composers, Richard and Jagger moved on to develop an entirely fresh repertoire concept for the Stones. Both *Time Is on My Side* and *The Last Time* were gold discs, but the Stones had yet to actually top the U.S. charts. The group's first runaway number-one smash would be a song recorded at a session in L.A. at the conclusion of the Stones' third American tour. *(I Can't Get No) Satisfaction* was a classic song of youth alienation in the mid-'60s and the disc that gave them a raging identity in North America.

Another distinctive Jagger-Richards song was *Get Off My Cloud*, a high-flying smash until radio stations discovered to their horror that the song was about a marijuana dream. The demon weed was becoming a highly controversial issue as more and more of us rejected alcohol and turned on with grass. In '64, the first year in which the F.B.I. began separate arrest statistics on marijuana, a total of 7841 Americans were arrested for possession. The following year arrests had increased almost 150 per cent, to 18,815 people.

By far the most significant arrival on the British rock scene in '65 was a group from south London called the Yardbirds, which would ultimately lead to the formation of Led Zeppelin. Like the Stones, the Yardbirds were discovered playing at the Crawdaddy Club by a former avant-garde French film-maker named Giorgio Gomelsky. The Yardies' first hit, *For Your Love*, was written by Graham Gouldman, a young composer from Manchester who would later join the Hollies and eventually 10 CC.

The year also brought an abundance of gimmick novelty records. The Kingsmen returned with an ad-oriented ditty about the *Jolly Green Giant*; Ireland's Ian Whitcomb whipped up a solitary hit with his pseudo-falsetto number, *You Turn Me On*; Shirley Ellis led the disco patrons through *The Name Game*; and Jonathan King moaned that *Everyone's Gone to the Moon*. The top-selling gimmick single of '65 came from Domingo Samudio, a Texan who dressed himself and his band in jeweled jackets with an Arabian flavor. They called themselves Sam the Sham and the Pharoahs and went all the way with *Wooly Bully*.

Hard R & B enjoyed notable success in '65, perhaps as a black reaction against the white rip-offs of rhythm and blues music. Many Top 40 radio stations which had previously turned a deaf ear to harder R & B sounds began to adopt a more progressive policy towards soul music. This loosening of the programming strings allowed R & B acts to reach back into their roots and rock up a storm. The mid-'60s were to be a prime period for sock-it-to-me soul. Wilson Pickett, former lead singer of the Falcons of Detroit, went back down to Memphis to record with the Booker T. Stax rhythm section. They cut a tune written by guitarist Steve Cropper that is a disco standard still—*In the Midnight Hour*.

The public seemed ready for the real thing, and artists like Otis Redding were just itchin' to give it to them. Otis had grown up in Macon, Georgia, the same area that produced Little Richard and James Brown. A dedicated admirer of the late Sam Cooke's singing style, he was signed by Stax Records in '63. After several potent blues records, Otis recorded a tune he'd written himself that would become one of the all-time greats of R & B—*I've Been Loving You Too Long (To Stop Now)*.

(Above opposite) Guitarists Jimmy Page (left) and Jeff Beck
(Below opposite) The inimitable Mick Jagger, shakin' it up
(Above left) early shot of Paul Simon and Art Garfunkel
(Above right) The "wicked" Wilson Pickett
(Below) haunting harmonies from the Mamas and the Papas

1965 saw the start of the disastrous U.S. military build-up in South Vietnam, a conflict that was to ultimately cost the American people the downfall of a president, the death of 56,000 Americans with 300,000 wounded, the killing of hundreds of thousands of North and South Vietnamese, and a still-to-be-healed division within the United States.

And so began the student protest era. At first the establishment spread the word that our dissent was communist-financed and infiltrated. We were, they insisted, traitors. But we simply didn't like the prospect of killing people for a cause for which we had serious and profound mistrust.

The polarization around heavy social issues in '65 was to have profound effect on the music industry. Artists began to develop a commendable sense of moral responsibility. Protest songs were, of course, far from new. What *was* new was rock's interest in subjects of more significance than straight-ahead romance. Undoubtedly drugs contributed to this intellectualization of rock. The music was no longer merely something to dance or cruise around to; now we were expected to get into the meaning of it as well.

Thus there began extensive cross-pollination of rock 'n' roll with authentic folk music, a union that would be invaluable to both forms as a young man named Robert Zimmerman would soon prove. At the start of the decade, Zimmerman packed his bags in Hibbing, Minnesota, and headed for Greenwich Village, where he planned to visit his ailing folk idol, Woody Guthrie. He hung around the Village, survived the winter by writing songs, changed his name to Bob Dylan, appointed Albert Grossman as his manager, and signed with Columbia Records.

Columbia had by now decided that rock was here to stay. *Bob Dylan,* his first album, was released in '62, the year that Bob wrote *Blowin' in the Wind.* The next year brought his first solo concert and the release of a second album, the brilliant *Freewheelin' Bob Dylan.* By now the subject of an intense cult following, Dylan became more withdrawn and introverted. He simply wouldn't commit himself; he wouldn't rush into anything. He had become suspicious of the intent of others. But his searing putdowns of the sick society in songs such as *Masters of War, A Hard Rain's Gonna Fall, Talking World War III Blues,* and *The Times They Are A-Changin'* invited critical acclaim and identification of Dylan as a spokesman for the alienated generation.

In '65 the folk singer and writer decided to electrify his music, to the horror of his purist folk following. He appeared at the Newport Folk Festival with a band of electric musicians, the Band, formerly the Hawks of Ronnie Hawkins fame. Electricity would make Bob Dylan accessible to millions with its classic union of folk and rock in *Like a Rolling Stone,* his biggest-ever single.

Rhythm and blues music, too, was discovering a conscience and looking to provide leadership. Little wonder, in view of the tragic riots in the L.A. ghetto of Watts. A minor arrest incident, and all the suppressed anger surged to the surface; more than 10,000 blacks took to the streets in what the authorities termed a "revolutionary uprising".

The teen genius himself, Phil Spector, Esq., was tied up in the studios with his latest protegés—Bill Medley and Bobby Hatfield, collectively known as the Righteous Brothers. The duo was not new, but it was felt that their success was long overdue. They'd released several minor hits through the Moonglow label in L.A. and had been notable regulars on the *Shindig* weekly rock TV series. But the really big breakthrough record had eluded them. Spector's first release on the Righteous Brothers was a song he'd written with Barry Mann and Cynthia Weill. *You've Lost That Loving Feeling* wrapped up the entire spectrum of love-lost ballads.

Paul Simon and Art Garfunkel weren't brothers either, but they'd recorded together in '57 as Tom and Jerry and landed a medium-sized hit with *Hey Schoolgirl.* In '64 Simon and Garfunkel were signed to Columbia Records, a label with an affinity for folk/rock music, since it had virtually no hard-rock acts. The duo recorded an album of gentle folk-flavored originals and called it *Wednesday Morning 3 A.M.* A perceptive producer took the vocal and acoustic guitar tracks of a song called *The Sounds of Silence,* adding a rhythm section of drums, bass, and electric guitar. The afterthought would boost Simon and Garfunkel to the top of the folk/rock ladder and establish them as the Everly Brothers of the '60s.

Generally acknowledged as the first of the folk/rock records, Bob Dylan's *Mr. Tambourine Man* was brilliantly interpreted by the Byrds. Most of their unique sound came from the jingle-jangle of Roger McQuinn's 12-string electric Rickenbacker guitar. The quality of their music elevated them to a position as America's most important new group but, sadly, the Byrds would never realize their true potential. Personnel problems, the pressures of stardom, volatile personalities — all of these factors contributed to the shortness of the Byrd's flight.

Eight Days a Week was the Beatles' opening number-one hit of '65. The John Lennon tune, *Ticket to Ride,* demonstrated the influence of Bob Dylan's work. It was obvious that the Beatles were having no difficulty in maintaining the unique position they'd carved out for themselves in American rock. In August the group was back on the road in the U.S. and Canada. Pandemonium accompanied every gig, and there were mob scenes of larger quantity and intensity than anything ever seen. The tour was launched with a spectacular outdoor concert at New York's Shea Stadium that represented the biggest gross in the history of show business.

John Lennon's tune, *I Feel Fine,* was especially significant as Lennon would later claim that the feedback at the beginning of the record was the first ever used intentionally on a rock 'n' roll record.

In Detroit the Motown sound was entering its fourth year on the charts, and Jr. Walker celebrated with his first million-seller *Shotgun.* Autry Dewalt Walker, the man who tore up on a tenor sax like never before, was the Motor City's first instrumentalist.

1965 brought another 4 Top-10 hits for the ever-amazing Marvin Gaye: *How Sweet It Is,* later to be revived by Jr. Walker and James Taylor; plus *I'll Be Doggone, Pretty Little Baby,* and *Ain't That Peculiar.* The mid-year of the '60s also marked the first of many million-sellers for the Four Tops, courtesy of course of the song-writing production trio of Holland, Dozier, and Holland — *Can't Help Myself.*

Predictably, the Supremes continued their spectacular chart activity with several more links in their historic chain of hits. The Supremes would ensure that Holland-Dozier-Holland had more hits on the American charts than any other composers, and that included Lennon and McCartney. 1965 was kicked off in notable style with the chart-topping *Come See About Me,* followed by *I Hear a Symphony* and *Stop in the Name of Love,* making it 6 number-one hits in a row.

Do You Believe in Magic, a John Sebastian song, was recorded by the Lovin' Spoonful, the first American East Coast group to challenge the supremacy of the West Coast white rock scene. The Spoonful had formed in New York's Greenwich Village in the early days of the folk boom. Their good-time music wasn't as raw or as raunchy as most of the British groups, but they provided a commercial link between the Beatles and the more biting Byrds.

Protest and social comment music continued to gain favor with the mass audience. The awareness of both artist and audience was expanding at an admirable rate. From swinging London, the Kinks introduced social satire to the charts with the brilliant Ray Davies song sending up the dubious values of social respectability. You could easily imagine a bowler-hatted man with brolly in hand making a charge for the morning train as the Kinks satirized *A Well Respected Man.*

A number of famous people ended their mortal lives in 1965, including Sir Winston Churchill, Albert Schweitzer, and Nat King Cole. Around the world, the establishment remained steadfastly committed to the technological dream. We were growing more and more skeptical of the way technology was being used without regard for the consequences. Our disenchantment took on broader dimensions towards the end of the year when the entire northeast seaboard was blacked out as a result of a relay breakdown in Niagara Falls. It was a big booboo for technology.

OTHER NOTABLE RECORDS — '65

MY GIRL — Temptations
HELP ME RHONDA — Beach Boys
CALIFORNIA GIRLS — Beach Boys
YESTERDAY — Beatles
LIGHTNING STRIKES — Lou Christie
TURN TURN TURN — Byrds
HANG ON SLOOPY — McCoys
EVE OF DESTRUCTION — Barry McQuire
PAPA'S GOT A BRAND NEW BAG — James Brown
A LOVER'S CONCERTO — Toys
I CAN NEVER GO HOME ANYMORE — Shangri-Las
HERE COMES THE NIGHT — Them
WE'RE GONNA MAKE IT — Little Milton
GO NOW — Moody Blues
POSITIVELY 4TH STREET — Bob Dylan
RESCUE ME — Fontella Bass
I DO LOVE YOU — Billy Stewart
TREAT HER RIGHT — Roy Head
NOWHERE TO RUN — Martha and the Vandellas
SHE'S ABOUT A MOVER — Sir Douglas Quintet
THE BIRDS AND THE BEES — Jewel Akens

1966

(Above left) The Beatles, strolling on top of the world
(Above right) a vital part of the Lovin' Spoonful, John Sebastian
(Below) The Stones rolling on the road again

1966 brought the first signs of a slow-down in the intensity of the British musical invasion. Or perhaps it was simply a case of American musicians mounting an effective campaign to re-establish Yankee leadership in the world of rock 'n' roll. Under pressure from Washington, American Top 40 radio stations began censoring rock lyrics to eliminate all records that even mentioned the subject of drugs, regardless of whether the song was for or against the alleged evils of drug use.

Summer in the City was one of the big summer hits of '66 by the pride and joy of Greenwich Village, the Lovin' Spoonful. One of the few songs to actually celebrate the urban existence, *Summer in the City* was just one of 4 million-sellers by the Spoonful in '66, the others being *Daydream, Rain on the Roof,* and *You Didn't Have to Be So Nice.*

Denny Doherty, Cass Elliot, Michelle Gilliam, and John Phillips had got together in Greenwich Village shortly after Bob Dylan's residence had made the area highly fashionable in folk circles. Later the 4 found themselves on the Virgin Islands with nothing to do but sing. The time they devoted to their group singing enabled them to work out complicated harmonies of a style unknown in rock. They signed with producer Lou Adler and were soon recognized as the fresh Pacific winds of change that rock had been looking for. John Phillips wrote both their first hit, *California Dreamin',* and the equally successful follow-up, *Monday Monday.*

There was a distinct folk influence on many of the West Coast produced hits of '66. Even format Top 40 stations weren't afraid to take a chance on the sort of records that would never have seen the light of day a year or 2 earlier. Bob Lind was an ideal example. His one and only outstanding original song, *Elusive Butterfly,* was a huge hit and paved the way for the acceptance of tunes by singer/song-writers such as Tim Hardin, Donovan and others.

The U.S. government pursued its policy of trying to put pot smokers in prison. In 1966 marijuana arrests had leapt up to 31,119, an increase of 70 per cent over the previous year.

Partly in response to the maturing of the Beatles on their latest album, *Rubber Soul,* and partly because of the influence of mind-expanding drugs, Brian Wilson was carefully taking the Beach Boys away from the great outdoors and inside the mind. The Beach Boys had always enjoyed a healthy respect with their superior harmony, but nobody was prepared for the release in May '66 of the Beach Boys' album tour-de-force, *Pet Sounds.* The LP contained 2 brilliant single hits in *God Only Knows* and *Wouldn't It Be Nice.* Then in the fall Brian Wilson unlocked the studio and let himself out with the master tapes of one of his all-time masterpieces, *Good Vibrations.*

In the spring the U.S. government made LSD, mescaline, and peyote, the key psychedelic drugs, illegal in an attempt to halt the coming drug craze. Professor Timothy Leary was raising gray eyebrows and consciousness levels across America with his advocation of LSD trips and his call for us to "tune in, turn on, drop out." We were more than ready. And so were countless rock artists who drew inspiration from their own life-styles to provide an account of the psychedelic in our music, acts such as the Electric Prunes, the Association, the First Edition, and Donovan.

Other political issues were bringing about a polarization of attitudes. We asked questions for which they had no answers. We were com-

Despite the British invasion, the Beach Boys (left) still hung high in the charts

Diversification was the new order of the day in rock and many heeded the call. Among them (above left) Yankee bubblegum Paul Revere and the Raiders; (above right) Master British minstrel Donovan Leitch; (below left) the Association applauded marijuana with *Along Comes Mary*; (below right) Percy Sledge put Muscle Shoals on the music map

ing to the end of the line, and the gap between parents and children had never been so visible. No writer of songs, prose, or poetry captured out bitter alienation quite so effectively as Pete Townshend, the lead guitarist of an up-and-coming British band called the Who. The Who spoke for all of us to the system when they screamed in *My Generation,* "Why don't you all just fu-fu-fu-fu-fade away!"

I Am a Rock was Simon and Garfunkel's contribution to explaining what it felt like to be alive in '66. The year also brought 3 other first-class singles by Paul and Art — *Homeward Bound, The Dangling Conversation,* and *A Hazy Shade of Winter.*

A total of almost 400,000 young Americans found themselves on foreign soil fighting an invisible and inexplicable enemy with the support of more than $200-billion worth of armaments and sophisticated weaponry. The U.S. force in Vietnam represented the most lethal array of killing power in history. But it was a new kind of warfare, and the GIs had little prior training in guerilla tactics. Things were going badly for the U.S., but it didn't surprise us. Our intuition had told us from the beginning that the Vietnam war was wrong. A broad anti-war political movement was finding a ready following among rock artists and audience. Ultimately it would divide the nation more bitterly and more decisively than any issue since the Civil War.

After 3 years of hard and fast rockin', Stevie Wonder dropped the "Little" and moved into a softer vein. His first gold single in '66 was a raunchy revival of Bob Dylan's *Blowin' in the Wind.* He then followed up with another smash, *A Place in the Sun.* Folk/rock was at the pinnacle of its power when Motown's master songsmiths, Holland-Dozier-Holland, picked up an unwritten challenge and set about creating the definitive folk/rock record utilizing the raw potency of soul music — the Four Tops' rendition of *Reach Out, I'll Be There.*

LBJ's highly publicized war on poverty had offered some long overdue hope to black people and other improverished Americans. But soon the have-nots discovered that the money allocated for their assistance had somehow been diverted to a more important purpose — the removal of the Red peril from Vietnam. The urban ghettos seethed with disappointment and frustration as black people sensed they had been led up the garden path. In 39 major urban areas, riots and the first stage of revolution flamed in the streets. The National Guard was called out to quash major disturbances in Chicago, Cleveland, and San Francisco.

For the young black, the only hope of escape from the ghetto was often success in either sports or music. Percy Sledge, a soul singer from Muscle Shoals, Alabama, showed just how far a black man could go. The Percy Sledge hit, *When a Man Loves a Woman,* would establish a cluster of 3 small towns, collectively known as Muscle Shoals, as an important rock production center.

A little further north, a conscientiously conservative black artist named Bobby Hebb was preparing an assault on the rock scene. Bobby had been the first black to perform at the Grand Ole Opry, the showcase of C & W talent, where he played spoons and sang with the Smokey Mountain Boys. At dawn of the morning following the assassination of John Kennedy, Bobby Hebb had composed an ode to optimism, *Sunny.* It couldn't have been more timely.

By October 1, Motown boasted 2 of the top 3 best-selling singles in the States, indisputable proof of its continuing dominance as the foremost independent rock label in rock music. Competitors spoke enviously of Motown's hot hit streak, but their success was due to much more than a simple lucky break. Each year since the start of the decade, Motown had increased its share of the rock market with black acts.

Rock was growing up and you could see the signs in '66 on the album charts, previously restricted to the schmaltz and syrup of MOR artists. Now such fine rock LPs as the Beatles' *Rubber Soul* and *Revolver, Aftermath* by the Stones, and Bob Dylan's *Bringin' It All Back Home* and *Blonde on Blonde* were among album best-sellers.

But the times were not changing rapidly enough for Phil Spector. Phil signed up the extremely funky R & B husband and wife team, Ike and Tina Turner. The Turners had made an impression on the rhythm and blues market earlier in the '60s and landed a half-million seller with *It's Gonna Work Out Fine.* Now Phil Spector put Ike and Tina together with a new song he'd written, *River Deep Mountain High,* then sat back and awaited Ike and Tina's arrival at number one. It happened almost overnight in England, but in the States, *River Deep Mountain High* stiffed at number 88 on the *Billboard* Top 100. After a miserable 4 weeks, it fell off the charts.

Spector, the genius of record production, was absolutely mortified. If the market wasn't hip

(Left)
Brilliant British hard rock band, the Spencer Davis Group, featuring the superb blues voice of Stevie Winwood (left)
(Right) Nancy Sinatra, boring but beautiful

enough to get behind his Ike and Tina masterpiece, then it would have to do without his talents. He announced his immediate retirement from the business. He would not return until 1969.

Back in Beatleland, the fab 4 were revving up for another spectacular year. The opening shot was the Paul McCartney song, *We Can Work It Out,* backed by Lennon's *Day Tripper* — their first double-sided million-seller since *I Feel Fine* and *She's a Woman* in late '64. The summer single, *Paperback Writer,* was a caustic Paul McCartney composition with some lyrical help from John Lennon. *Yellow Submarine* was written by both; the other side, *Eleanor Rigby,* was Paul's melody with mainly John's lyrics. John and Paul were still close enough to collaborate. However, though no one knew it then, the Beatles were passing their prime as a group. Their final public appearance together had taken place on August 29 in Candlestick Park, San Francisco.

Meanwhile, the Rolling Stones maintained an outrageous image of unadulterated rebellion. At times their determination to be the bad boys of rock led to hysterical confrontations with the system. The Jagger-Richard original, *19th Nervous Breakdown,* was the sixth gold single for the Stones. September brought the single, *Have You Seen Your Mother Baby Standing in the Shadow,* but the Stones' biggest hit of '66 was a heavy track from the new *Aftermath* album, *Paint It Black.*

In England, a singer/song-writer named Donovan Leitch, who'd scored 3 minor hits with anti-war songs, changed direction and producers and emerged with his first walkaway number-one smash, *Sunshine Superman.* He followed it with another of his own distinctive songs, *Mellow Yellow.*

The first head shops began to open in the main streets of America as we searched for an alternative to the mass consumer society. Ancient Egyptian temples at Abu Simbel were saved from the encroaching waters backed up by the Aswan Dam on the upper Nile. Andy Warhol's *Chelsea Girls* opened in New York.

OTHER NOTABLE RECORDS — '66

UPTIGHT — Stevie Wonder
(YOU'RE MY) SOUL AND
   INSPIRATION — Righteous Bros
COOL JERK — Capitols
AIN'T TOO PROUD TO BEG — Temptations
WHAT BECOMES OF THE BROKEN
   HEARTED — Jimmy Ruffin
EIGHT MILES HIGH — Byrds
ALONG COMES MARY — Association
NOWHERE MAN — Beatles
IF I WERE A CARPENTER — Bobby Darin
SUMMERTIME — Billy Stewart
RAINY DAY WOMEN — Bob Dylan
WILD THING — Troggs
HOLD ON I'M COMING — Sam and Dave
BABY SCRATCH MY BACK — Slim Harpo
I HAD TOO MUCH TO DREAM LAST
   NIGHT — Electric Prunes
WALK AWAY RENEE — Left Banke
BLACK IS BLACK — Los Bravos
I'M YOUR PUPPET — James and Bobby Purify

1967

The Beatles, back in Liverpool for publicity pix to promote *Penny Lane* (right) while the Stones (over) stayed home and sought satisfaction in assorted shapes and sizes

1967— the year when change would sweep through the rock 'n' roll scene, bringing with it unforeseen developments in the basic structure of records and radio. 1967 would also see the blossoming of flower power and the love-peace-grooviness ethic that first drew inspiration from the streets of Haight-Ashbury in San Francisco. It was a period of extreme sensitivity, when young people the world over would make one last try at saving the world from a grim future of pollution, over-population, and the debris of the industrial revolution.

Penny Lane, Paul McCartney's song, was one side of the Beatles' first single in '67. Both *Penny Lane* and the flip side, John Lennon's brilliant *Strawberry Fields Forever*, presented the Beatles in a new setting. It was their thirteenth number-one hit, but it didn't appear to put any jinx on the follow-up, which would be introduced to the largest audience in the history of TV or music. The BBC produced a global TV special celebrating the age of Telstar communications and the possibility of international unity. In June '67, hundreds of millions of people all over the world tuned in their tubes to watch the Beatles deliver a prophetic message to mankind, *All You Need Is Love*. The lads followed it to the top of the charts with a Paul McCartney tune entitled simply, *Hello Goodbye*.

Meanwhile, Britain's bad boys of rock were having a tough time getting any sort of exposure. The problem was a new Stones single called, rather bluntly, *Let's Spend the Night Together*, their fourteenth single and their least successful to date.

Gimme Some Lovin' was the breakthrough record in America for the British group whose home popularity was exceeded only by that of the Beatles and the Stones. For a brief time, the Spencer Davis group would compete for the Stones' American audiences, but because of singer Stevie Winwood's fragile health, lengthy tours were out of the question.

Procol Harum would take rock music in an entirely new direction with one of the most progressive singles in British rock history. *A Whiter Shade of Pale* represented an unlikely combination of a Bach cantata entitled *Sleepers Awake*, a guitar player named Robin Trower, superb surrealistic lyrics, a Latin name that meant "beyond these things", and the aching organ sound and unique vocals of Gary Brooker. A one-in-a-million record, it was the sort of single that was impossible to follow. Rather than get hung up behind it, Procol Harum soon moved into the forefront of the progressive album scene. The time was fast approaching when singles would no longer be absolutely vital to the continuation of a musical career.

Another British artist developing a cult following on albums in the aftermath of one big single was Van Morrison. After his Belfast-based group, Them, disbanded, Morrison moved to New York at the invitation of writer/producer Bert Berns. In Manhattan, he wrote a tune called *Brown-Skinned Girl*, which he then changed to *Brown-Eyed Girl* in view of likely broadcast controversy over mixed romances. Despite this bowing to commercial interest, some radio stations were also offended by the lyrics of *Brown-Eyed Girl* and censored out the line, "Making love in the green grass behind the stadium."

Never My Love represented more gold for the Association out of L.A. The rock audience had never seemed so receptive to soft ballads. Across the continent in the Big Apple, the Young Rascals did a total turn-around away from the storming rockers that had launched

(Above left) Aretha Franklin teamed up with Atlantic and launched a spectacular and long overdue career
(above right) Michael J. Pollard in the anti-hero youth film hit, *Bonnie and Clyde*
(below left) Van Morrison, highly acclaimed lead singer of Them
(below right) Linda Ronstadt, voice of the Stone Poneys

their career. Their new vehicle was a super-moody Felix Cavaliere and Eddy Brigati original, a song that would always seem so right on a lazy summer's day — Groovin' on a Sunday afternoon.

The Letter, number-one smash for the Box Tops from Memphis, sounded like so many great oldies rolled into one. It was that familiar hook line, that catch phrase that caught your attention and would roll back into your mind again and again. The Letter was a textbook exercise in what hit records were about.

In a way, the Doors were initially Hollywood's answer to the Stones. Lead singer Jim Morrison was a sometime poet of the L.A. high life who appeared ready to give absolutely everything to his music. He came on hot and heavy in the sexual sense, as Mick Jagger had done. The songs specified and invited fierce bodily contact, the music was highly repetitious, and both Doors and Stones geared themselves to the task of turning on young girls. But the Doors also had an organ player who underlined Morrison's growling vocals with a stream of orgasmic sound. With Morrisons' song, Light My Fire, the doors to the charts were opened very wide.

June brought the beginnings of what the mass media would call the summer of love. Those cynical war children were giving love another chance, and this time it was for real. Somehow the first sparks of idealism had found a home in the Haight-Ashbury district of the Bay City. Scott McKenzie came through with the marching song for all those West-Coast-bound in the summer of '67; "If you're going to San Francisco, be sure to wear some flowers in your hair."

San Francisco would be a catalyst for creative endeavor and 1967 saw the launching of Rolling Stone magazine in the Bay City. It was also the time and place for the introduction of so-called FM underground radio, which aimed to satisfy the tastes of an adult rock audience. One of the first of the San Francisco bands to explode across America was the Jefferson Airplane. The Airplane flew high with 2 gold singles in '67, Somebody to Love and White Rabbit.

There could be no doubt that San Franciso was the key center of the youth culture in America in the late '60s. But Los Angeles wasn't going to go down without a stiff fight. For a start, L.A. was less of the love, peace, and grooviness and more of the anger and discontent of youth. And there was obviously a need for both outlooks. As the story went, the Buffalo

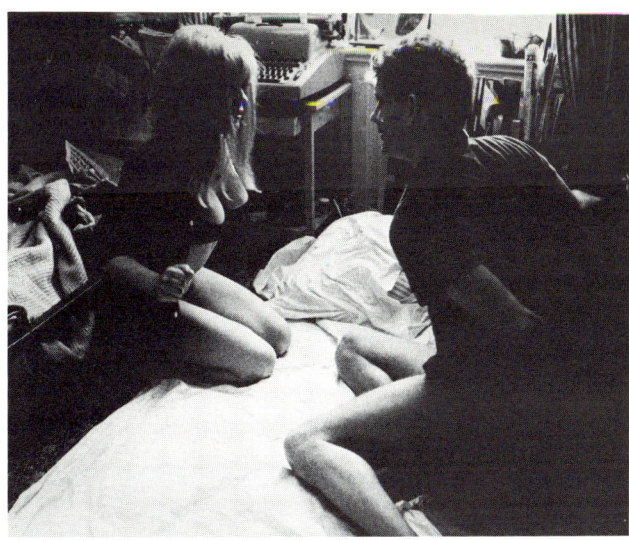

I Am Curious Yellow, landmark film in the fight for cinema freedom against censorship

Springfield had been formed after 2 singer/guitarists, Steve Stills and Richie Furay, had met a couple of Canadian expatriates, bass player Dewey Martin and the singer/guitarist Neil Young, in the parking lot of an L.A. shopping plaza. In a grinding climate of domestic division and rising anger between young and old, hawk and dove, black and white, haves and have-nots, the Buffalo Springfield hit the nail right on the head with the Steve Stills classic protest song, For What It's Worth.

The news was grim and getting grimmer. While war in Vietnam raged, the Arabs and Israelis plunged into the Six-Day War. When the dust settled, the Arabs were in a state of disarray and the planet was again on the threshold of nuclear war.

Three U.S. astronauts were burned alive on the launching pad at Cape Kennedy after their spaceship exploded because of technical faults. At least 66 people were killed and 3000 injured in another outbreak of bitter racial violence in Newark and Detroit. The establishment had begun to react to try to temper black violence. The first black Supreme Court Justice, Thurgood Marshall, was sworn in.

But the threat of the draft was the big fear in all young hearts and minds. We were against that war, and we were damn sure we didn't want to go over there killing people in a cause we didn't support. The war was *their* war. If the Pentagon wanted to wipe out the North Vietnam commies so badly, let them do it themselves. On October 21 and 22, the first major anti-war protest demonstrations took place in Washington. Thirty-five thousand protesters turned out to bum rap an unjust war. LBJ would remain unmoved.

It was a memorable year for soul music. Arthur Conley, who had been discovered by Otis Redding, served up disco dynamite with his hit, *Sweet Soul Music*. Redding was still looking for that pop hit for himself, but it would not arrive until after his triumphant appearance at the Monterey Pop Festival and the tragic event of December '67. Shortly before Christmas, Otis Redding was on tour with the Barkays; their chartered plane crashed near Madison, Wisconsin, and all on board perished.

In Memphis, Sam Moore and Dave Prater were already associated with the soul classic, *Hold On, I'm Comin'*. Then they took the Stax sound straight to number one with a tune written by Isaac Hayes and David Porter, laying down the hard facts about a *Soul Man*.

After Atlantic Records' producer Jerry Wexler arrived at Muscle Shoals, the recording center would quickly achieve world-wide fame. He suddenly turned up in Muscle Shoals looking for a spot of southern inspiration and was so impressed that he soon returned with an ex-gospel singer named Aretha Franklin. Ms. Franklin had spent 5 fruitless years recording for Columbia, which had been unable to uncover the right direction for her. Wexler took Aretha to a funky studio across the Jackson highway from a cemetery and made musical history for Muscle Shoals with her first big hit, *I Never Loved a Man*. Aretha Franklin would, from these humble beginnings, become the best-selling female singer in the history of recorded music.

Dylan fans were shocked when news of Bob's serious motorcycle accident in Woodstock hit the headline. The problem was lack of news about the accident, and in the absence of any definite details, all sorts of grisly rumors went the rounds. Dylan was near death, crippled, a mindless vegetable, finished with music forever. Nobody knew what to believe, and the stories multiplied. One thing seemed certain — Bob Dylan really was out of action.

Romantic folklore took a pounding when the South African surgeon, Dr. Christian Barnard, performed the world's first heart-transplant operation. The patient would live for 18 days. In the meantime, the heart was fast losing its legendary status as the center of all matters concerning love and romance.

I Can See for Miles was the first U.S. million-seller for the Who, featuring singer Roger Daltrey and guitarist/song-writer Pete Townshend. Although their American success was slow in coming, the Who were quickly gaining acceptance as one of the most exciting and important rock bands in Britain.

After 3 months of long studio sessions, the Beatles emerged in June with what was unquestionably their finest musical achievement thus far. The growing band of rock critics would not take long to label *Sgt. Pepper's Lonely Hearts Club Band* as the rock album of the decade, a masterpiece of musical construction and ingenuity. With a title song written by Paul McCartney, *Sgt. Pepper* would demonstrate the individual diversification of Beatle members in the aftermath of their massive success—after they'd had a little time and a lot of drugs to ponder upon themselves.

Sgt. Pepper was a suite of songs, rather than the usual odd collection of tracks clustered together at random to fill 12 inches of vinyl. The album possessed an over-all concept and structure that would have much bearing on the evolution of album music. But to some fans, the Beatles seemed to be deserting rock 'n' roll. You couldn't deny that the Beatles, with a little help from friends such as producer George Martin, were in the process of taking their music into a broader context. *Sgt. Pepper* was by any definition an album of classic pop music, and it showed how far rock could reach. The Beatles' genius was shining through as never before.

OTHER NOTABLE RECORDS—'67

RESPECT—Aretha Franklin
RUBY TUESDAY—Stones
I WAS MADE TO LOVE HER—Stevie Wonder
PURPLE HAZE—Jimi Hendrix Experience
BY THE TIME I GET TO PHOENIX—Glen Campbell
HIGHER AND HIGHER—Jackie Wilson
I HEARD IT THROUGH THE GRAPEVINE—Gladys Knight and the Pips
I SECOND THAT EMOTION—Miracles
GIMME LITTLE SIGN—Brenton Wood
WOMAN WOMAN—Union Gap
EVERLASTING LOVE—Robert Knight
COLD SWEAT—James Brown
I'M A MAN—Spencer Davis Group
BACK UP TRAIN—Al Greene
A NATURAL WOMAN—Aretha Franklin

1968

1968—rock music moved into an intense period of diversification. It's hard to believe that so many assorted sounds could achieve hit status.

In the spring, the pride of the Big Apple came through with one of their finest records — *A Beautiful Morning*, the fifth million-seller for the Rascals. Now they'd dropped the "young" from their name and were gaining international acclaim with the follow-up. Shortly before the Russians invaded Czechoslovakia to prevent further liberalization of that country, the Rascals insisted that *People Got to Be Free*. It would be their last Top 10 hit. Later in '68 they began to move away from the dynamic simplicity that had marked their earlier hits, and it wasn't long before they'd lost touch with the shifting sands of public taste.

Elsewhere in New York, the giant Columbia Records conglomerate was finally making a connection with the rock record market through its newly appointed president, Clive Davis, a lawyer who shrewdly manipulated Columbia's image from one of MOR wholesomeness to that of a sympathetic radical corporation. With Davis at the top and Mitch Miller sent out to pasture, where he could grow corn instead of recording it, Columbia set about restoring its credibility with the contemporary record market. Davis had attended the Monterey Festival in '67, and this led to the signing of several new, with-it acts, including Janis Joplin, the Chambers Brothers, and Sly Stone.

Simon and Garfunkel's first big hit of '68 was their lush treatment of the traditional folk ballad, *Scarborough Fair*. But it was *Mrs. Robinson*, the theme song from the movie, *The Graduate*, that would really establish Simon and Garfunkel as folk/rock superstars.

There could be no doubt that '68 was one of rock's best years. Some of the finest sounds thus far produced would find their way to the top of the charts. Some of them came from highly unlikely sources — few more unlikely than the British actor, Richard Harris, and his first astounding entry into the rock music field, *MacArthur Park*. Jim Webb not only wrote the masterpiece, but arranged and produced it as well. Although it was over 7 minutes long, *MacArthur Park* was a massive AM hit. Usually Top 40 stations only play records of around 3 minutes, but with an instant classic like *MacArthur Park*, exceptions were made.

Meanwhile, our attention continued to be focused on the planet's predicament. Nuclear war loomed on the horizon briefly when an American intelligence ship the *Pueblo*, and its crew of 83 were captured by North Korean patrol boats in communist waters. The crew remained in North Korean jails until 2 days before Christmas. They returned home as heroes, although the communists denounced them as spies.

The world was profoundly saddened by yet another assassination on American soil. Martin Luther King, the civil-rights leader, was brutally shot to death in Memphis. His killer, James Earl Ray, escaped and was not captured until many months later, halfway around the world.

In February Richard Milhous Nixon announced his candidacy for the Republican presidential nomination, and a month later John Kennedy's brother, Bobby, announced that he would seek the Democratic nomination. And a succession of earthquakes crunched through western Sicily, causing damage of millions of dollars.

Few groups of the late '60s had more interesting backgrounds than Steppenwolf. Originally called the Sparrow, the group had started in Toronto with lead singer, John Kay, a German-born lad with a liking for black leather. They were managed by Stan Freeman, the entrepreneur who had made a fortune from the Electric Circus disco in New York. When Canada's music scene failed to make them millionaires, Steppenwolf moved to the States, where they soon took off with *Born to Be Wild*, the song

(Left) No singer anywhere could compare with the raw ferocity and authentic blues of Otis Redding. It was a tremendous tragedy when Otis was cut down in his prime by an untimely air crash

Simplicity took a commercial surge forward with San Francisco's Creedence Clearwater Revival (above)

Mick Jagger continued to be the number-one front man in rock, but his starring role in the Australian film, *Ned Kelly* (right) did little for his rock reputation.

(Opposite right) Janis Joplin, a white lady who lived the blues
(Opposite left) Jim Morrison, lead singer of the Doors
(Below left) One of the final Beatles publicity pix, released to accompany the single Hey Jude
(Below right) A rainy afternoon in London's Carnaby St (credit: Yorke)
(Above) A rare picture of the Bee Gees (or brothers Gibb) starting out down under.

composed by organ player Goldie McJohn, who would also write Magic Carpet Ride and Rock Me, 2 other Steppenwolf hits.

After a 4-year absence as a heroin addict, Dion Dimucci returned to the AM scene in '68 with a song that brought a tear to the most cynical eye — Abraham, Martin and John, the story of Abraham Lincoln, Martin Luther King, John Kennedy, all public servants who were gunned down.

And the killing had not ended. In Los Angeles in June, Robert Kennedy was assassinated by a man described as an "Arab fanatic". The official story was that Sirhan Sirhan was trying to get back at Bobby Kennedy for backing American support of Israel in the Middle East conflict. It didn't seem like the good old U.S.A. anymore. Three men who'd promised change had been gunned down in 7 years, just the way things were supposed to happen in those South American banana republics. We envisioned a tomorrow where politicians drove around in tanks and lived in underground chambers near their beloved missiles.

Frustrated by the total scene and unable to gain any degree of control over how they were being educated, students at Columbia University in New York started a mass riot. For a time they occupied the Dean's office, a symbolic victory. But even more violent confrontation was to take place in Richard Daley's city of Chicago during the Democratic convention. Thousands of young people from all over America came to Chicago to express their complete disgust at the way the country was being run. Angry at the nerve of these protesters, Mayor Daley unleashed the city police in one of the most violent attacks upon the public ever seen in the United States.

The Chicago convention and police brutality against protesters would prove to be a turning point in American history. The battle positions had been drawn up. Even the mass media, whose members had felt the clout of police clubs in Chicago, now felt sympathy and rapport with the counter-culture. A profound disenchantment with politics was slowly spreading to older liberals. In fact, the war had proved too much for Lyndon Johnson. He announced that he would step down and not contest the presidential election. He'd had enough of the nonsense and of our dissent.

Sly and the Family Stone were exciting exponents of a new kind of rhythm and blues music that might be best termed psychedelic soul. Inspired by a variety of artists, including Jimi Hendrix, Ike and Tina Turner, and the Temptations, Sly Stone and his family hit the million mark first time out with Dance to the Music. They would be one of San Francisco's most prominent AM acts into the '70s.

One of the truly great soul records of '68 was Clarence Carter's Slip Away. And one well-known person who slipped away for a surprise wedding was Jackie Kennedy, widow of the assassinated president. Jackie was joined in holy matrimony with the Greek shipping magnate, Aristotle Onassis. Six days later the Republican presidential candidate, Richard Nixon, scored a narrow victory of a bare .07 per cent of the popular vote over Hubert Humphrey, thus becoming the 37th president of the United States. Nixon had promised that he would listen to and support "the voice of the great majority of Americans, the forgotten Americans, the non shouters, the non demonstraters that are not racists or slick, that are not guilty of the crime that plagues the land."

Rock was redirecting its energies in the album field, for several key reasons. Albums allowed extensive innovation, impossible within the confines of a 3-minute song. With the increased scope of an LP, an artist could hope to project a definite image and a message. It was really the difference between a newspaper and a full-length book in terms of musical approach. Furthermore, record royalties were a lot higher on LP sales than on singles.

The growing popularity of a small and intimate concert hall circuit was making it easier for an act to become popular without radio play. Such clubs as the Fillmores, East and West; the Kinetic Circus in Chicago; Boston's Tea Party; the Rock Pile in Toronto; and L.A.'s Whisky à Go Go gave valuable exposure to new acts. They sold albums, too. And sometimes these albums would open up to reveal smash hit singles from left field. It took a year to break, but Cream finally landed a massive single with a track from the best-selling LP, *Disraeli Gears*, entitled *Sunshine of Your Love*.

The ever-Rolling Stones were back on top early in '68 with *Jumping Jack Flash*. A week after its release, they announced with notable glee that the highly respected French film director, Jean-Luc Godard, would be committing the Stones to celluloid in a documentary entitled *Sympathy for the Devil*. The follow-up to *Jumping Jack Flash* was a track from the forthcoming *Beggars Banquet* album called *Street Fighting Man*. It was a song about revolution, and many U.S. radio stations, fearing further rioting, kept it off their playlists. Mick Jagger commented, "I'm rather pleased that they have banned *Street Fighting Man* as long as it's still available in the shops. The last time they banned one of our records in America it sold a million." With Mick it was business as usual.

The Beatles had taken a low profile and were into the mystical trips of the Maharishi, but there was no shortage of British bands working an act up for the American market. The glimmers of future trends and hit acts could be seen in London's recording studios, if you knew where to look. After the Yardbirds broke up, lead guitarist Jimmy Page plunged into a hectic session-playing career, which soon made him the most in-demand young guitarist on the scene. One afternoon he was hired by a bass player named John Paul Jones to work on a new single by Donovan; the session would produce a gold disc, *Hurdy Gurdy Man*, and the start of a significant relationship between Page and Jones to be explored further in Led Zeppelin.

1968 was to be a significant year for the success of both authentic black blues and white versions thereof. Cream had paved the way for new bands to experiment upon blues themes as

The highly effective union of Art Garfunkel (right) and Paul Simon reached its zenith with *Bridge Over Troubled Waters*

they'd done with Robert Johnson's *Cross Roads* and Willie Dixon's *Spoonful*. Dozens of other British groups did their own arrangements of standard blues tunes by Muddy Waters, B.B. King, Elmore James, and other black legends. They earned fortunes from album sales and packed concerts, playing black man's blues the white way. Rock music had gone back to its taproot of the blues for inspiration. We were back in an era of simple 12-bar blues, performed for the mass market.

But not all British acts were into blues, and not all British-sounding groups were really British. The 3 Gibb brothers—Barry, Maurice, and Robin—were born in Manchester, but their family emigrated to Australia in '58. After getting together a teen record act down under, the Bee Gees (for Brothers Gibb) figured they'd made a mistake in leaving England. Back 'ome, they recorded a bunch of original tunes on which their vocals tended to sound remarkably like the Beatles. The Bee Gees hit the magic million mark with their seventh single, the Barry Gibb ballad, *I've Got to Get a Message to You*.

Paul McCartney's clever putdown of religion, *Lady Madonna*, was the Beatles' first single of '68, but when it came out, they weren't around to promote it. The lads were halfway around the world in India trying to suss out the Maharishi, who knew how to get high *without* drugs. They reunited in London to launch their Apple group of counter-culture companies. Tired of being contracted to established show-biz corporations, they wanted to put some of their own money into creating an alternative to the giant corporate music- and film-makers. Apple's first Beatles single, a double-header combining Paul's *Hey Jude* with John's *Revolution*, became the biggest hit thus far in the group's career, surpassing even the red-hot '64-'65 period.

Altogether, '68 was a lively year for the Beatles. In July Lennon hosted the world premiere of the progressive cartoon film *Yellow Submarine*, for which the Beatles provided several original songs. In August, Paul McCartney delighted millions of young women around the globe by calling off his engagement to Jane Asher. In November, Cynthia and John Lennon obtained a divorce, and less than a month later John and his new lady, Yoko Ono, presented themselves on the jacket of an album cunningly called *Two Virgins*. The jacket showed John and Yoko in the nude, full frontal shots. American record distributors refused to stock the album, so *Rolling Stone* magazine ran the nude picture as a special centerspread. John and Yoko were well on their way to becoming the world's most famous couple.

Motown was still go-town in the charts in '68, the year Marvin Gaye hit number one for the first time with his moody revival of the Gladys Knight hit of the previous year, *I Heard It Through the Grapevine*. Stevie Wonder consolidated his glittering career with a series of gold hits — *Shoo-Be-Doo-Be-Doo-Da Day*, *For Once in My Life*, and *You Met Your Match*. The Temptations, too, were boiling hot, dishing up their sixth million-seller with yet another stunning Norman Whitfield-Barrett Strong original, *I Wish It Would Rain*.

One of rock's most exciting young stars first hit the charts in '68. Janis Joplin had enjoyed a meteoric rise after joining the San Francisco band, Big Brother and the Holding Company, in '66. Then came a spotlight role at Monterey Pop and her sudden signing by Clive Davis at Columbia Records. Janis recorded a tune that had been an R & B hit for Aretha Franklin's sister, Erma Franklin, the year before. *Piece of My Heart* would be her first big single and the launching pad for a brief but often glamorous career.

The lovely former gospel singer from East Orange, New Jersey, Dionne Warwick, notched up her 23rd consecutive hit, the million-seller *Do You Know the Way to San Jose?*, another winner from the composing team of Hal David and Burt Bacharach.

Despite the rain and misinformed U.S. intelligence reports, the North Vietnamese launched the Tet offensive in the middle of the monsoon season. It would be the first in a series of stunning reversals for the American-supported Diem regime. The G.I.s had all the big guns, but the Viet Cong seemed to have the spirit of the people. American bombers poured down a stream of steel on the North Vietnamese territory, but no matter how severe the bomb damage, the Viet Cong would have it repaired within weeks.

On Broadway, a raunchy play celebrating the ethic of love, peace, grooviness, and long hair, full of nudity and 4-letter words, was packing them in at every performance. *Hair* would soon revolutionize the theater world, which had done its best to ignore the first 15 years of rock music.

Billboard magazine named Aretha Franklin as the top singles artist of the year, the first time that a woman had ever received the honor. Lady Soul was also the number 12 album artist of '68, indicating the inroads made by R & B into the long-play scene. Aretha landed one hit after another from the Miami studios, working with the Muscle Shoals rhythm section. She followed the Goffin-King song, *A Natural Woman*, with *Chain of Fools*, *Since You've Been Gone*, *Think*, and then a stunning revival of Dionne Warwick's *I Say a Little Prayer*.

Otis Redding had played a role in Aretha's career by writing what was probably her best-known song, *Respect*. In 1968, the year after his death, Otis Redding himself had 6 chart hits, including his one-and-only number-one record, the pensive original *(Sittin' on) The Dock of the Bay*.

OTHER NOTABLE RECORDS — '68

TIGHTEN UP — Archie Bell and the Drells
LIGHT MY FIRE — Jose Feliciano
LA LA MEANS I LOVE YOU — Delfonics
SAY IT LOUD (I'M BLACK AND I'M PROUD) — James Brown
ITCHYCOO PARK — Small Faces
THE TIME HAS COME TODAY — Chambers Bros
IN-A-GADDA-DA-VIDA — Iron Butterfly
HUSH — Deep Purple
SPOOKY — Classics IV
STONED SOUL PICNIC — 5th Dimension
THE MIGHTY QUINN — Manfred Mann
WHITE ROOM — Cream
SWEET INSPIRATION — Sweet Inspirations
HEY JUDE — Wilson Pickett

1969

A cast of superstars:
(above left) Keith Richard of the Stones (credit: Annette Carter)
(above center) The Bob Dylan "comeback" picture
(above right) Brian Jones, ill-fated founder of the Stones
(below) George Harrison at Apple, '69 (credit: Annette Carter)

1969—the final year of the '60s and a period that could only be an anti-climax after the grim events of the previous year.

Proud Mary was the first of 9 consecutive million-selling singles for an unknown group from the San Francisco Bay area who called themselves Creedence Clearwater Revival. It was in a sense a return to rockabilly roots — simple, basic 3-chord rock 'n' roll that everybody could relate to.

The Doors were maintaining what could only be called a prominent profile. Jim Morrison had become a star of *16* magazine, much to the horror of the group's underground following, but he swiftly regained his counter-culture credibility during a March concert in Miami. Florida police issued 6 warrants for his arrest on charges involving "lewd and lascivious behavior in public by exposing his private parts and by simulating masturbation and oral copulation" during the Miami concert. Not surprisingly, the new Doors single, released to capitalize on the Miami rap, was entitled *Touch Me*.

By the end of the '60s, everybody seemed to be capitalizing on the protest era, even Elvis Presley. Elvis scored his first certified million-seller since '63's *Bossa Nova Baby* with *In the Ghetto*, a protest song written by an aspiring singer/song-writer named Mac Davis. It was part of an album entitled *Elvis in Memphis*, the King's first non-film-track album in several years.

Presley's career had settled on a plateau of sorts by the end of the '60s. While he was still a legend, his music didn't appear to have much appeal for the young record-buyers. It was just too mushy and MOR-oriented for a generation weaned on the Beatles, the Stones, and the Doors. But the King kicked off the cobwebs in '69 and re-established his teen credibility with *In the Ghetto*, followed by another million-seller, *Suspicious Minds*.

One of the most highly acclaimed album groups of the late '60s, the Band were a key factor in spearheading a Canadian mini-invasion of the U.S. charts in this period. They'd backed up Ronnie Hawkins in Toronto in the mid-'60s, and then Bob Dylan persuaded them to accompany him on the controversial electric tour that introduced folk audiences to folk/rock. After recording several albums with Dylan, in '68 the Band introduced their own debut LP, *Music from Big Pink*, named for the house where they'd rehearsed in Woodstock, New York. There were no singles from *Big Pink*, but the second album produced the classic track, *Cripple Creek*, which was written by guitarist Robbie Robertson.

Another musician from Toronto who met with enormous American success was the white blues singer, David Clayton Thomas. In '69, Thomas was asked to replace Al Kooper as vocalist with the New York jazz/rock band, Blood, Sweat and Tears. The first album with Al Kooper had not been a big seller, but the union with David Clayton Thomas yielded a landmark album and 4 hit singles — among them, *You Made Me So Very Happy*. It was a pioneer record, demonstrating what could be done when musical barriers were shot down by powerful talent.

A number of gold singles came from the score of *Hair*, including Three Dog Night's *Easy to Be Hard*. *Good Morning Starshine* by Oliver, the Cowsill's *Hair*, and the number-one seller of the entire year, *Aquarius*, as sung by the 5th Dimension.

The political scene was in its usual state of turmoil. The Chicago Eight trial quickly descended into a courtroom farce, a battle of wits between radical and rigidly conservative. In light of what had come out about the corruption within the Chicago police force, many of us considered the trial an establishment hoax.

The extent of corruption around the core of the establishment began to reveal itself when Supreme Court Justice Abe Fortas was forced to resign over questionable business dealings. Warren Burger was installed as Chief Justice

Bag Productions Inc.
Tittenhurst Park,
Ascot, Berkshire.
Ascot 23022

9th December 1969

The Rt. Hon. P. Trudeau,
Prime Minister,
Government of Canada,
Ottawa.

Dear Prime Minister,

As per our telephone conversations with your various aides we are pleased to inform you that we shall be arriving in Toronto next Tuesday and shall be staying for at least a week.

We look forward to the opportunity of meeting with you during that time and would be pleased if your office could try to arrange an appointment at your convenience.

Pursuant to this we are asking Messrs. John Brower, Richard Miller and Ritchie Yorke to contact your office and to look after the necessary arrangements.

We look forward very much to seeing you.

Love and peace.

John Lennon
Yoko Ono Lennon

John and Yoko Lennon

Rock discovers a conscience with John and Yoko Lennon's WAR IS OVER IF You Want It peace mission. The couple were welcomed to Canada by Prime Minister Trudeau and stayed at Ronnie Hawkins' farm near Toronto. (left to right) Rompin' Ron, wife Wanda, John and Yoko and America's concerned comedian, Dick Gregory. (credit: Annette Carter)

Pop festivals were the rage of the late '60s as part of a back-to-Nature trend. Woodstock was the biggest of all. Joan Baez (below left) fared well with an audience anxious to throw off the yoke of tradition and inhibition. Even Quebec superstar Robert Charlebois (right) tried for an English following at the Toronto pop festival.

and conservatism was on the rise. The acute problem of planet over-population was recognized for the first time in a presidential address to Congress.

It was a painful year for concerned conservationists. The massive Santa Barbara oil spill washed hundred of thousands of gallons of oil upon the beaches of California, wiping out much wildlife. Scientists warned that the chances of further oil spills increased every day as more and more tankers were being put into service to transport the life-blood of the technological society. On Europe's Rhine River, insecticide caused the deaths of some 40 million fish. Wherever you looked, our natural resources were being eaten up in the name of progress.

The late '60s marked the return of one of the original Memphis rockabilly singers, Johnny Cash. (Y'all remember *Ballad of a Teenage Queen* and *I Walk the Line*.) Johnny had attached himself to a new audience by identifying with less fortunate minorities. In '68 he recorded a notable album in concert behind the walls of Folsom Prison, and in the last year of the '60s he came through with the first million-selling single of his 14-year career, *A Boy Named Sue*. Everybody was into doing their own thing at the end of the '60s. The Isley Brothers scored with *It's Your Thing*, while most of Britain's superstar guitar players would readily admit that *their* music was really B.B. King's thing. No other black blues musician had so influenced rock music in the latter '60s. His style of playing and his knack of stretching the strings at the neck of his guitar had detonated the explosion of blues rock. From Indianola, Mississippi, B.B. King had begun recording in '49 and enjoyed minor success in the R & B market through the '50s and '60s. Then a whole generation of British guitarists began to imitate B.B.'s style with immense success. Eric Clapton was one of them. Finally, 20 long years after entering the record industry, B.B. came through with his first giant pop hit, the spine-tingling blues ballad, *The Thrill Is Gone*.

Although we didn't know it then, the Beatles' single of Paul McCartney's rock revival tune, *Get Back*, contained a certain prophetic message. The song had been recorded up on the roof of the Apple building, just a stone's throw from Piccadilly Circus, the hippie heart of London. It was to be part of the *Let It Be* movie, and it was also a last attempt at rejuvenation within a jaded group. It was also the last public appearance by the Beatles, although the audience consisted

Led Zeppelin founder Jimmy Page (*credit: Annette Carter*)

only of curious office workers and a handful of Apple scruffs, plus the film crew.

In July and August, the Beatles' last recording sessions as a group took place at the Abbey Road studios in London. In September the new album, *Abbey Road*, was released, and it rocketed to number one. Named after the EMI studios in North London where most of their hits had been recorded with producer George Martin, *Abbey Road* was a masterpiece by any definition. From the album came *Something*, George Harrison's tune that was to be the Beatles' last single of the '60s and the first one on which a Harrison song had been accorded an "A" side.

The Beatles had frequently credited Bob Dylan with influencing their music, and they were among his most prominent fans. After a long and arduous recuperation from his Woodstock motorcycle accident in '67, Dylan reappeared at a Johnny Cash concert and cut an album in a new direction, *Nashville Skyline*. It was an album of love songs. It seemed that now Bobby was ready to retire from the protest scene and get down to a little lovin'. *Lay Lady Lay* was his first hit single in over 2 years.

1968 was a memorable year in the space race, the year in which Apollo 11 carried astronauts Michael Collins, Edwin Aldrin Jr., and Neil Armstrong to the moon. Without doubt the moon flight and landing was a tremendous victory for technology and a breakthrough on the frontiers of science. But somehow the timing was all wrong. At the time, millions of earthlings didn't know where their next meal was coming from; 30 per cent of the U.S. populace was living at starvation level.

Perhaps the most heartening news for hardened rock fans was the return of production genius Phil Spector. Phil emerged from a self-imposed 2-year retirement to produce the lead singer of a popular West Coast club act called the Checkmates Ltd. The singer's name was Sonny Charles, and Spector connected him with an outstanding song entitled *Black Pearl*.

Green River was the third consecutive smash hit for Creedence Clearwater Revival, fast becoming America's most popular rock group. Of course, the competition was intense. The front ranks included an extremely commercial band from Los Angeles known as Three Dog Night. The group featured 3 alternating lead singers and specialized in recording the cream of current songs; they didn't write their own material. 1969 brought them 3 million-sellers: the Randy Newman tune, *One; Easy to Be Hard*, from *Hair*; and the superb Laura Nyro song, *Eli's Coming*.

Although Three Dog Night ultimately would outlast Creedence, they were never to gain favor with the so-called underground audience, mainly because the group did not create its own material. Song-writing was becoming extremely important; many critics judged a band's potential purely on the strength of the original material it offered.

The Stones came up with a classic rock 'n' roll record, Keith and Mick's *Honky Tonk Women*. But as it happened, honky tonk women would be the least the Stones had to worry about in '69. In May Mick and his girl-friend, Marianne Faithful, were busted, the same day that Mick announced he'd accepted the starring dramatic role in a film about the legendary Australian bushranger-highwayman, Ned Kelly. A couple of weeks later, guitarist Brian Jones — an original member of the Stones since '62 — shocked the music world by announcing his decision to leave the band. It was, he said, the result of a clash with Mick Jagger. Twenty-four days later he was found dead in the swimming pool of his Sussex manor-house.

At the end of the Stones' '69 American tour — their first in 3 years — Mick Jagger made the gravest mistake of his career — one that would haunt him forever. In a display of incredible naiveté Jagger okayed the hiring of a pack of Hell's Angels to supervise security during a free concert in Altamount, California. In a scene of ugly violence, a black youth was murdered by a member of the Hell's Angels. The rock generation, still glowing in the memories of 3 days of historic peace and music at Woodstock, were shocked.

A multitude of superstars had been assembled in a farmer's field in upstate New York by the promoters of the Woodstock Festival. The line-up included Joni Mitchell, Jimi Hendrix, Ritchie Havens, Joan Baez, Joe Cocker, the Jefferson Airplane, Ten Years After, Sly and the Family Stone, and Crosby, Stills, Nash and Young. More than 400,000 music freaks turned out for a belated celebration of love, peace, and grooviness. It was to be the largest gathering for peaceful purposes thus far in the history of mankind. The Who were among the sensational successes at Woodstock, and one of their best-received tunes was a track from their new rock opera concept album, *Tommy* — *Pinball Wizard*.

John and Yoko in turn unveiled the Peace Festival, featuring the giants of rock appearing for the ultimate cause, peace and goodwill. It seemed too good to be true. And we got right into the groove when Led Zeppelin, an incredible new British hard rock band laid down some of the greatest sounds of the '60s. One of the most significant records of '69 was their *Whole Lotta Love*, an essay in discord and alienation reduced to raw and potent sexual terms.

Assembled late in '68 by ex-Yardbird guitarist Jimmy Page, Led Zeppelin had within a year of their formation risen to superstar ranks faster than any band since the Beatles. Despite put-downs by rock critics, Led Zeppelin appeared to have filled a vacuum vacated by an increasingly introverted Jimi Hendrix and a curdled Cream. As the screaming '60s screeched to a close, Led Zeppelin was the top-selling record act in the world.

OTHER NOTABLE RECORDS — '69

EVERYDAY PEOPLE — Sly and the Family Stone
IN THE YEAR 2525 — Zager and Evans
THE BALLAD OF JOHN AND YOKO — Beatles
GIVE PEACE A CHANCE — Plastic Ono Band
THESE EYES — Guess Who
CLOUD NINE — Temptations
OH HAPPY DAY — Edwin Hawkins Singers
HE AIN'T HEAVY — Hollies
EVERYBODY'S TALKIN' — Nilsson
THE BOXER — Simon and Garfunkel
CAN I CHANGE MY MIND? — Tyrone Davis
GET TOGETHER — Youngbloods
I STARTED A JOKE — Bee Gees
25 MILES — Edwin Starr
WHAT DOES IT TAKE — Jr. Walker
GAMES PEOPLE PLAY — Joe South
UNDUN — Guess Who
WHEN I DIE — Motherlode
LEAVING ON A JET PLANE — Peter Paul and Mary
I GOT A LINE ON YOU — Spirit

1970

The '70s dawned under new rock leadership, that of the intrepid Led Zeppelin featuring vocalist Robert Plant, drummer John Bonham and guitarist Jimmy Page.

1970, the first year of a new decade, and happy birthday sweet 16 for rock 'n' roll. The winds of change were blowing strong as rock grew up and institutions fell apart.

A sensational new white blues singer from Sheffield, England—Joe Cocker—hit the charts with his rendition of Paul McCartney's *With a Little Help from My Friends* from *Sgt. Pepper*. Cocker had a little help from studio friends like Jimmy Page on lead guitar, drummer B.J. Wilson, and keyboard player Stevie Winwood.

An exciting new band who landed a number-one single with their first release featured Paul Rodger, Simon Kirk, Andy Fraser, and Paul Kossoff. Together they called themselves Free and *All Right Now* would free them from many hassles as it stormed to the top. British hard rock bands had the American scene bewitched with heavy blues. They dominated the scene as the Beatles had done in the mid-'60s. For a time it seemed as if being an American band was the kiss of death with U.S. rock audiences.

It wasn't easy, but emerging U.S. rock bands such as Chicago Transit Authority and Santana overcame the stigma of not-being-British by breaking through via the Top 40 scene. Chicago was a horn-oriented group which owed at least some of its inspiration to the jazz/rock giants, Blood, Sweat and Tears. Their producer, James William Guercio, had worked with BS&T until conflicting egos had soured the relationship. Guercio then moved to Chicago and connected with one of the foremost American rock bands of the '70s. *Make Me Smile* was Chicago's first gold single, and they followed soon after with *25 or 6 to 4*.

At the beginning of the '70s there was no shortage of acts aspiring to cater to young teens. Even Motown — which by now had moved away from race-torn Detroit to the more secure clime of California—was ready to take a shot at the bubblegum market. The Jackson 5 were a fantastic combination of funk and fantasy, soul and bubblegum — 5 young black guys whose vocals were highlighted by the superb Motown production sound. *I Want You Back* was the first of 4 number-one smashes for the Jackson 5, proving that the bubblegummers had the bucks to back up their musical preferences.

Another big bird born to fly in the first year of the '70s was the jumbo jet, Boeing's extension of the 707. The 747 did not travel much faster than the 707, but it carried more than twice the passengers and cargo, thus allowing greater profits. Never mind that ground-handling facilities couldn't cope with the jumbos. The 747 would be a huge financial success for Boeing.

The comeback-of-the-year award belonged without doubt to Tony Orlando. After 3 moderate hits in the early '60s, Tony quit performing and became a record promotion man. His chance to return to the spotlight came when he was asked to sing on a demo disc of a new song called *Candida*. Even greater success was in the air for the ex-song-writer and demo record singer. The follow-up to *Candida* was a song that soared past the million mark and topped charts around the world — *Knock Three Times*.

Never slow to catch onto a bandwagon, the major record companies viewed the success of soft hits such as *Close to You* and *Raindrops Keep Fallin' on My Head* as an indicator of a crumbling of rock. And there still remained an industry bias against hard rock. Record labels that had been trying to get to grips with heavy metal suddenly made a switch and moved into the softer mold. Record companies were convinced that there was big bread to be made from the softer sound. If Top 40 would give exposure to soft rock singles, then it was time for a flood of them. One such came about when a singing song-writer named David Gates put together a vocal group appropriately named Bread and set about trying to *Make It with You*.

In the aftermath of the unsettling '60s, there appeared to be a temporary emotional lull. It was hard to be optimistic. The new American

It was a new decade but the same old faces prevailed in rock.
(Opposite upper left) Ronnie Hawkins celebrated his rediscovery by John Lennon with a visit to Rome's Coliseum (credit: Yorke)
(Opposite upper right) Paul McCartney announced the breakup of the Beatles a few days before launching a solo career
(Opposite below) Stephen Stills, on the run from the Nixon regime, moved to Surrey mansion in England to ride horses and to lose his favorite Gibson guitar (credit: Yorke)
One notable new face (with lots of hair) was Elton John, budding British superstar (left)

way was demonstrated once again when the entire family of Joseph Yablonski, an unsuccessful candidate for the presidency of the United Mine Workers Union, was found shot to death in Clarkesville, Pennsylvania. And still Congress would not look favorably upon any proposals to disarm its disaffected citizenry.

Guns were okay, but grass was still taboo in America. The first year of the '70s saw the arrest of 188,682 citizens on marijuana charges, an increase of almost 70 per cent over 1969.

Paul McCartney's song, *Let It Be*, was the Beatles' first single in the '70s and the second last of their career. When the new year rolled around there was very little previously recorded material in the can. Lennon and McCartney couldn't cope with the idea of working together again in the studio, so eventually the tapes from the abandoned *Let It Be* album were pulled from the vault. Beatles' U.S. business manager Allen Klein persuaded Phil Spector to have a crack at putting the album together. The trouble was that John and Paul were so uninterested that neither showed up for even a few minutes at the London studio where Phil was adding masses of string sweetening and mixing the tracks.

John and Yoko were getting into some weird things, among them the cult of magic and the psychiatrist who specialized in primal therapy, Dr. Janov. All of these trips led to the release of the somewhat peculiar Plastic Ono Band single entitled *Instant Karma*, John Lennon's first million-seller as a non-Beatle.

Canada had become the heaviest country of the hip world. It was here that John and Yoko launched their last peace campaign, in the process meeting with Prime Minister Trudeau, Marshall McLuhan, Dick Gregory, and the erotica publisher, Ralph Ginzburg.

On April 10, Paul McCartney announced that he had no further plans for recording with the Beatles, and newspapers around the globe headlined the break-up. Ringo, who'd been suspicious about the group's future the longest, was the first to hit the market with a solo album. The McCartney album hit the street 2 weeks later. George began work on his solo album in May with producer Phil Spector.

In America, Capitol Records released its final Beatles single, a Paul McCartney song, *The Long and Winding Road*. It would be the Beatles' 31st million-selling single. No act in the history of show biz had ever quit so far ahead of its decline.

And no rock act captured the complex mood of these turbulent times as brilliantly as Paul Simon and Art Garfunkel in *Bridge Over Troubled Water*. It was a masterful reflection of a world in total disarray. In March the U.S. army accused 14 officers of involvement in suppression of information about mass killings of civilians at Song My in South Vietnam. The My Lai relations would follow. In neighboring Cambodia, Prince Sihanouk was overthrown as head of state. Several commercial airliners were hijacked by guerilla groups hoping to gain media attention. A French submarine with 37 crew members failed to surface after a practice dive in the Mediterranean. China launched its first unmanned satellite into space.

The Canadian government banned commercial fishing in Lake Erie because of high mercury content in fish. In the British elections, Edward Heath's Conservative government scored a victory over the Labour team led by Harold Wilson. In Washington Nixon announced that, at his instructions, U.S. troops had attacked communist bases in eastern Cambodia. As the times got tougher and tougher, a segment of young people turned to a variety of religions to try to find what it all meant.

A Ball of Confusion, that's what the world is today, sang the Temptations, and who could deny it? The Temptations had it down as it really was, and the greening of Motown was a landmark event in the history of rock. Company policy had long prevented Motown acts from discussing touchy topics, such as politics, with the media. In the explosion of dissent in the late '60s, Motown's policy had become a laughing-stock with the underground press, but in the new decade, Motown artists suddenly burst forth with a wave of funky protest hits. Norman Whitfield and Barett Strong would prove to be the most effective song-writing team in this style. Marvin Gaye would also make heavy contributions. Putting down the white establishment was suddenly *in* at Motown, and lyricists set about telling it like it was. Edwin Starr followed his '69 gold single, *25 Miles*, with a classic number-one raver about the horrors of *War*.

By now Crosby, Stills, Nash and Young were virtually the hottest group in America, considered by many to be the successors to the Beatles. Their hit single, *Woodstock*, came from a 2-million-selling album entitled *Déjà Vu*, a brilliant album that took 800 hours to record. Crosby, Stills, Nash and Young lived in the canyons of Los Angeles and were bitterly critical of American politics. So it came as no surprise when the band's singing guitar player, Neil Young, wrote an angry song—*Ohio*—about one of the most tragic events in American history, the shootings at Kent State.

The level of anti-war protest demonstrations had reached fever pitch. Campuses were ablaze with anti-war philosophy. Angry, alienated children of the Bomb had simply had enough. And then at Kent State University, May 4, in a chilling blunder National Guardsmen shot and killed 4 student protesters. It was one of the saddest days America had ever known.

The political scene was too much for Crosby, Stills, Nash and Young. They turned their backs on superstardom and took off on a search for peace of mind. David Crosby and Graham Nash set out on a long boat trip; Neil Young returned to Canada before resuming a solo career; and Steve Stills bought himself a plane ticket for London.

Settling down in England, Steve Stills based himself at a splendid 16th-century manor-house in Surrey owned by Ringo Starr. It wasn't long before he was back in the studios, slogging away at a debut solo album with an impressive array of celebrity guests, including Eric Clapton, Ringo Starr, and Jimi Hendrix. It was obvious that this was not to be yer average, run-of-the-mill first solo album by a former group member. Steve Stills was recognized as one of the foremost talents in rock, and AM stations jumped right on a track from his new album, *Love the One You're With*.

Another album-oriented artist to break through into the singles scene this year was James Taylor, soon to become one of America's most prominent singer/song-writers. Taylor's first album had been recorded in London in '68 for Apple Records, with Peter Asher acting as producer. Taylor's relationship with Apple went nowhere, but Asher and Taylor teamed up in L.A. to produce an album for Warner Bros. It wasn't long before a single from that album took the charts by storm. It was called *Fire and Rain*.

One of the left-field surprise hits of the year was a further example of the diverse nature of contemporary music. It was the 200th anniversary of the birth of Ludwig von Beethoven, the great classical composer. To commemorate Ludwig's musical genius, a Spanish heart-throb named Miguel Rios took the "Ode to Joy" finale from Beethoven's beautiful Ninth Symphony and turned it into an anthem of love, peace, and joy. *Song of Joy* was a tribute to the durability of Beethoven's music and message.

There could be no doubt that the Guess Who were the most successful rock group ever to emerge from the north country — Canada — fitting tribute for the group, their manager Don Hunter, and producer Jack Richardson. And there was lots more to come. The new decade brought even greater glories for the Guess Who, including their first American chart-topper, the runaway smash, *American Woman*, written by singer Burton Cummings and lead guitarist Randy Bachman. But shortly after the *American Woman* triumph, Randy Bachman left the line-up to form his group, Brave Belt. Soon after Bachman's departure, the Guess Who released a new single entitled *Share the Land*, which topped the million mark despite being banned as "communistic" by several southern stations.

As Canadian hits soared on the U.S. charts, thousands of alienated young Americans headed north to seek refuge in a neutral country. Labeled draft dodgers, these emigrants were in fact on the run from the oppression of the U.S. system as much as the Vietnam war. Ironically, Canada made no effort to deter U.S. draft dodgers from pouring across its borders, yet all the while continued to supply arms for use by Americans in Vietnam.

It was hard to contest Three Dog Night's case as America's number-one singles group. They'd scored solidly with several records — though not their own compositions — in '69, but 1970 brought their first number-one hit, a rousing rocker written by Randy Newman called *Mama Told Me (Not to Come)*.

With *Someday We'll Be Together* the Supremes chalked up their 12th number-one hit and 17th million-seller, but Diana Ross hankered to begin a solo career. Her first single, *Reach Out and Touch Somebody's Hand*, was a moderate success, but the follow-up, *Ain't No Mountain High Enough*, rocketed to number one. Diana Ross was definitely ready to go it alone.

Elton John's first American single, *Border Song*, had been notably unsuccessful, but Aretha Franklin's rendition of Elton's tune, following up on her gold revival of Ben E. King's *Don't Play That Song*, fared much better than the original. Throughout most of 1970, Elton John was still an unknown.

Ouside American borders, the scene was grim. Hardly a week went by without a major air crash or a hijacking. Arab guerillas scored bonus points when they blew up a 747 jumbo jet at Cairo Airport. The British Trade Commissioner in Montreal, James Cross, was kidnaped by the Quebec Liberation Front. Cross was later released unharmed, but Quebec guerillas murdered the provincial Minister of Manpower, Pierre LaPorte.

A cyclone and ensuing tidal wave smashed into East Pakistan, killing between 200,000 and 500,000. Starvation loomed in Biafra, and there were military coups in Argentina, Bolivia, and Syria. On his first southeast Asian tour, Pope Paul escaped injury in an assassination attempt in Manila by a knife-wielding Bolivian.

In America 2 blacks were killed and 9 wounded in a disturbance at Jackson State College, and the Chevron Oil Company was fined one million dollars in New Orleans in a case deriving from the company's massive oil pollution of the Gulf of Mexico.

As the year shuddered to an end, England's Elton John finally found the right single to launch his American career. *Your Song* was a masterpiece of simplicity from the pens of Elton and his lyricist, Bernie Taupin. The first year of the '70s had seen the demise of the Beatles but it had also marked the arrival of Elton John. We didn't fully realize it then, but the reins of rock had been passed along.

OTHER NOTABLE RECORDS — '70
DOWN IN THE ALLEY — Ronnie Hawkins
IN THE SUMMERTIME — Mungo Jerry
THE TEARS OF A CLOWN — Miracles
THE LETTER — Joe Cocker
NO TIME — Guess Who
MISSISSIPPI QUEEN — Mountain
SIGNED SEALED DELIVERED I'M YOURS —
    Stevie Wonder
CALL ME — Aretha Franklin

1971

Canadian singer/song-writer Gordon Lightfoot finally gained that vital foothold on the American AM charts with *If You Could Read My Mind* (credit: Annette Carter)

1971, and rock music had become one of the most influential cultural media of the 20th century. Dollar-wise, it had exceeded the annual grosses of the movie and TV industries and was still going gangbusters as the audience expanded. By now there was a clear demarcation between the single and album-buying audiences. FM radio had gained a strong foothold in many markets, but AM didn't appear to be hurting. The rock audience now spanned the age groups from 8 to 30.

By 1971 the voice of protest had reached a crescendo. From the dead-end depths of the ghetto, from what remained of the proud Indian tribes on the reservations, from the shabby shanties of southern field hands, from the alienated offspring of the affluent middle class — from the hearts and minds of everyone who gave a damn burst forth one over-riding question, given voice by Marvin Gaye: "Just what the hell is going on here, man? When we look at the world it fills us with sorrow; little children today are really gonna suffer tomorrow." Marvin Gaye's question rang out loud and clear. Most important, *What's Going On* represented the greening of the blues. The music that had spawned rock 'n' roll was moving into the universal protest cause. Soul music was getting to grips with the Predicament.

Cat Stevens, the outstanding new British singer/song-writer who'd torn the album charts apart with his *Tea for the Tillerman* LP, came through with some timely advice — Come on and climb aboard that *Peace Train*.

God rock reached its zenith with the stupendous success of a rock musical recreation of the life and times of one Jesus Christ — *Jesus Christ Superstar*, written by 2 young Englishmen, Tim Rice and Andrew Lloyd-Webber. At first religious leaders were offended by the irreverence, but it didn't take them long to work out that the message was the medium. *Jesus Christ Superstar* would do more for the revival of religion than a million broadcasts of Oral Roberts or Billy Graham.

The year also saw the launching of a record career by a former Memphis song-writer named Isaac Hayes, who had helped to write *Soul Man*, among others, for Sam and Dave. He landed his debut number-one hit as a performer with the theme from the black movie, *Shaft*.

Riders on the Storm would be the last hit for the Doors. The storm of success proved too much for lead singer and cult celebrity, Jim Morrison. He was found dead in a bathtub in Paris on July 3 with a trace of a smile on his face. It was the third rock tragedy of the early '70s, following on the deaths the year earlier of Jimi Hendrix and Janis Joplin, both from drug overdoses.

Within a year of her death, Janis Joplin had found the hit single she had failed to connect with during her life. The tune was written by an emerging Nashville song-writer named Kris Kristofferson, a former Oxford student. *Me and Bobby McGee* would ensure that Janis Joplin would not be forgotten.

Drugs became an obsession with the U.S. government. Law officers who would have been better occupied trying to reduce the Mafia's influence on American society stepped up the campaign to frighten us away from drugs. Almost a quarter of a million Americans were arrested in '71 for marijuana offenses, an increase of about 25 per cent over the previous year. The U.S. broadcast licensing authority, the F.C.C., again informed all stations that they would be encouraging drug use by programming any lyrics mentioning dope. That edict covered a lot of records. Obviously, dope was an important part of the rock culture, and the music only served to report and remind us where it all was coming from. Rock lyricists

(Opposite upper left) Carole King creating *Tapestry*
(Opposite upper right) Budding female singer/song-writer Carly Simon
(Opposite below) Lady Soul was an appropriate title for rock's all-time top selling female vocalist, Aretha Franklin
(P. 145, upper) Led Zep's Jimmy Page
(Center) Marvin Gaye who brought about the greening of the blues
(Lower) Van Morrison, vintage rock genius

naturally wrote about drugs, because dope was commonplace part of the rock life-style — indeed, the youth sub-culture.

One of the very few artists who was genuinely not into drugs was Van Morrison, the expatriate Belfast singer/song-writer. His biographer claims that Morrison stopped taking all drugs and alcohol in 1970 and has not resumed since. Van Morrison's '69 album, *Astral Weeks*, had been universally acclaimed as one of the great masterpieces of rock. It was a concept album — there were no songs suitable for singles, and as a result *Astral Weeks* received very little AM play. Two albums further on and Van Morrison came through with a big hit single, with his band and Street Choir and his own song, *Domino*.

On the bubblegum scene, format bands such as Paul Revere and the Raiders kept grinding out pretty much the same old stuff. They had a field day catering to the sub-teen singles market. But they'd been around for a decade now, and lacked the youthfulness of other emerging teen acts. *Indian Reservation* would be Paul Revere's last big hit with the Raiders.

The "old" pre-teen acts were being replaced by a new breed of even younger artists, such as the Jackson 5 and the Osmond family. The first month of '71 brought the Osmonds the first of many golden hits, *One Bad Apple*. The reasons for the success of the Osmonds were obvious. A new generation of record buyers found it difficult to relate to the "old men" of rock — the Beatles, the Stones, and Simon and Garfunkel. Those guys were almost old enough to be their fathers.

It was a long road to Carole King's first hit. Her real name was Carol Klein. Neil Sedaka had written *Oh Carol* about her, and along with her first husband, Gerry Goffin, she'd written a bunch of the '60s most durable songs—*Will You*

145

Still Love Me Tomorrow? for the Shirelles; *The Locomotion* for their babysitter, Little Eva; *On Broadway* for the Drifters; and *A Natural Woman* for Aretha. 1971 proved that Ms. King was equally talented as a performer. With producer Lou Adler, who'd worked with the Mamas and Papas, Carole cut an album called *Tapestry* which included the *It's Too Late* single. Both the album and single went to number one, and *Tapestry* would ultimately become one of the top-selling LPs in rock industry.

After a comparatively quiet '69, the Bee Gees blasted into the '70s with 2 million-sellers, *Lonely Days* and *How Can You Mend a Broken Heart?*, the latter their first American number one. The Bee Gees had certainly come a long way from Brisbane, Australia. Their other million-seller of '71, *Lonely Days*, was another brilliant production of an original tune by the Gibbs brothers.

On the news front, Charles Manson and 3 young women were found guilty of murdering actress Sharon Tate and 6 others. Major James Chichester-Clark resigned as prime minister of Northern Ireland in the wake of continuing religious riots. Brian Faulkner was selected to replace him in one of the world's most undesirable jobs.

A leering lad and a lusty singer, Rod Stewart had tried numerous gigs before connecting with the group called the Faces. When they were known as the Small Faces with Steve Marriot as lead singer, the band had scored many hits in Britain, but only one or 2 in America. Rod Stewart's first solo album, *Gasoline Alley*, yielded a double-headed smash, the Tim Hardin tune, *Reason to Believe*, coupled with is own original, *Maggie May*.

An education in how to put together a near-perfect commercial single came from a former British session musician named Dave Edmunds. In '71 Edmunds dressed up an old Fats Domino hit from '61, *I Hear You Knockin'*, with all the trimmings of the '70s. And after 15 hit singles, Ike and Tina Turner finally landed their first million-seller with that powerhouse revival of the Creedence classic from '69, *Proud Mary*.

The kings of British rock 'n' roll were still the Stones, ever rockin' and ever rollin'. 1971 was the year in which they found themselves in Britain's 97 per cent tax bracket. And so, like latter-day Somerset Maughams, they packed off and found tax shelter in the south of France. Relocated on the French Riviera, Mick Jagger married Bianca Rosa Perez-Mora, former girlfriend of actor Michael Caine and society daughter of a Nicaraguan diplomat.

Early in summer the Stones launched their own record label through Atlantic, ending a long and bitter association with the conservative Decca/London label. The new label was called, naturally enough, Rolling Stones Records. The album was titled, almost as predictably, *Sticky Fingers*. From its Freudian packaging came the Stones' first new single in almost 2 years; its title, *Brown Sugar*, referred to a variety of cocaine.

The biggest Beatle hit since the group's break-up was written and recorded by George Harrison. When the group had split, pop pundits had predicted that John and Paul couldn't miss as solo artists but that George and Ringo would have a harder time. Here now was George, the up-and-coming composer who'd had hassles trying to get his tunes recorded by the Beatles, coming through with the biggest ex-Beatle hit of '71. *My Sweet Lord*, with melody line remarkably similar to the Chiffons' '63 hit, *He's So Fine*, came from Harrison's triple album, *All Things Must Pass*, produced by Phil Spector.

Paul McCartney didn't use Spector, but he wasn't doing so badly by himself, along with a few friends, wife Linda, and an outstanding number-one smash that brought back all the flavor and feeling of Paul's finest moments with the Beatles: *Uncle Albert/Admiral Halsey*. Even Ringo, with the help of Phil Spector, came through with a gold solo record, *It Don't Come Easy*.

Meanwhile, *Rolling Stone*'s man of the year, John Lennon, who'd been expected to emerge as the biggest solo star from the Beatles, had a sluggish start with *Power to the People*, a highly political statement about democratic idealism. Realizing that romance was a more commercial subject, Lennon released *Imagine*, one of the few non-political tunes from his new album.

1971 was to be peak year for Three Dog Night. They notched up 3 gold singles, beginning with a triple million-seller, folk-singer Hoyt Axton's tune, *Joy to the World*.

In March, Lieut. William Calley was found guilty by a court martial of premeditated murder of at least 22 South Vietnamese civilians at My Lai in 1968. He was sentenced to life imprisonment, a living example of what racism and lack of moral integrity could do to young soldiers. Ultimately Calley served a short sentence in better conditions than the majority of American workers. He was housed in an apartment with meals supplied, and he was even allowed to entertain his girl-friend in the evenings.

One of the most macabre rock acts of the '70s, Alice Cooper demonstrated the importance of hit singles with a record called *18*. It launched the son of a mid-western preacher as one of the most unusual and shrewdly managed entertainers in rock history. To liven up his concert act and to establish a unique image, Alice added drama, in the form of snakes and gallows, using various props to encourage fantasizing. He believed that the rock audience feasted on its fantasies, and his tremendous success indicated that he was right on. The music, Alice felt, was of much less importance, and he proved that, too, by using session musicians on most of his records.

For years Gordon Lightfoot had been Canada's most popular homegrown entertainer, and he'd been steadily building up a stong U.S. folk-cult following through weekend college dates. His link to the American mass market came through the title track of Gordon's first album for Warner Bros., *If You Could Read My Mind*.

Prior to entering the music scene, Bill Withers had worked for the Boeing Aircraft Corporation, assembling toilet seats. In '71 he came up with a classic slice of soul, *Ain't No Sunshine*.

The women's movement gained momentum in 1971. The establishment had been discriminating against women since time immemorial, so it really was no surprise that women decided they'd had enough.

On the political scene, police continued to wield the big stick at protesters. More than 12,000 demonstrators were arrested during the May Day protest in Washington, then released, most of them uncharged. Only 79 demonstrators would be convicted out of the 12,000 arrests. Walter Hickel, one of the few politicians who demonstrated any sort of concern for the future of the environment, was fired by Nixon for, among other things, criticizing the U.S. invasion of Cambodia.

In July Nixon shocked "better-dead-than-Red" conservatives when he announced that he would make a formal visit to the People's Republic of China within the next 9 months. In September, a wild and brutal police assault on rioting prisoners in New York's Attica State Prison resulted in the tragic deaths of 33 inmates and 9 guards. In London, where belligerent Irish terrorists had taken to blowing up civilian targets as a reprisal against Britain's military presence in Northern Ireland, emergency measures were taken to protect the Queen en route to the opening of Parliament.

Despite massive anti-radiation protest from around the globe, the Nixon government went ahead with a 5-megaton nuclear explosion beneath Amchitka Island, probably to demonstrate to the North Vietnamese what might lie ahead for Hanoi. Nixon also faced a mounting storm of media protest about his conduct of the Vietnam war after a disaffected federal employee named Daniel Ellsberg leaked the Pentagon papers to the *New York Times*.

America and the world were in the grips of a getting-back-to-nature kick, instigated by alienated young people and concerned elders. The backlash against technology and the chemical society would continue to grow through the '70s as more and more of us tried to find escape from a corporate, mass-consumer society. Communes had gained favor in recent years, and an increasing number of young city folk were trying their luck on the land.

Lady Soul, Aretha Franklin, made a stunning gold-disc revival of Simon and Garfunkel's classic of the year before, *Bridge Over Troubled Waters*. It was Aretha's tenth gold single and a return to the fantastic form that had made her the best-selling female recording artist in history. The year also produced a remarkable live album by Aretha and Ray Charles in concert together at Fillmore West. But Fillmore owner, Bill Graham, announced that greedy rock groups had forced the closing of his New York base, the Fillmore East in Greenwich Village.

Britain's fast-rising solo star, Elton John, followed up his *Your Song* success by combining with lyricist Bernie Taupin to write the musical score for a movie entitled *Friends*. The title song was a moderate hit, but nowhere near the success of the first track pulled from Elton's fourth album, *Madman Across the Water* — *Levon*.

OTHER NOTABLE RECORDS — '71

AIN'T NO SUNSHINE — Bill Withers
TIRED OF BEING ALONE — Al Green
ONE TOKE OVER THE LINE — Brewer and Shipley
I WON'T GET FOOLED AGAIN — Who
SPANISH HARLEM — Aretha
IF — Bread
GROOVE ME — King Floyd
ISN'T IT A PITY? — George Harrison
BRIDGE OVER TROUBLED WATERS — Aretha Franklin

1972

Elton John, by now emerging as a significant showman and prolific melody maker

1972—the year that will always be remembered for Don McLean's classic record, *American Pie*, and for the re-election of Richard Milhous Nixon. In '72 the younger rock audience greatly influenced the AM Top 40 scene—witness the soaring singles success of the Osmonds and the Jackson 5. Album artists had gone in another direction, and many of the top-drawing acts in rock were by now rarely, if ever, heard on AM airwaves.

Never had rock albums and singles been so far apart. The most popular request song on American radio for the whole year was a track from Led Zeppelin's fourth album, *Stairway to Heaven*, which was not even released as a single. There were 2 main reasons for this—producer/guitarist Jimmy Page would not consent to any editing of the tune from its original 8-minute length, and Zep preferred the larger revenues from album sales. If you wanted *Stairway to Heaven* in your collection badly enough, Zeppelin figured you'd go out and buy the LP.

In the AM field, soul music had become a prime influence on record sales. Black had never been more beautiful to Top 40 programmers. Eric Burdon's former backing group on *Spill the Wine*—War—emerged on their own with the first of several smash soul/pop hits, *Slippin' into Darkness*.

The renaissance of R & B also brought about the re-emergence of Philadelphia as a major American recording center, as it had been in the late '50s. A pair of writer-producers named Kenny Gamble and Leon Huff set up shop in the City of Brotherly Love and proceeded to launch the Philly International label. Their first success was with a veteran R & B vocal group called the O'Jays, who'd been recording since '63 and notched up 10 minor R & B hits, the best known of which was *Lipstick Traces*. But they rocketed to the top with *Backstabbers*.

Not only Philly was staging a big comeback to the world charts. Memphis, too, was getting some very mean sounds together. The Staple Singers were a well-known folk/gospel group who had gathered a cult following on the folk-festival circuit in the late '60s. Their concert repertoire included several Dylan tunes, and the group had actually recorded the original version of the Rolling Stones smash, *The Last Time*. The Staple Singers signed with the Stax/Volt label, and their fourth single, *I'll Take You There*, took them to the million-sales milestone.

Winner of the seventh annual Rio Song Festival was David Clayton Thomas, who received the celebrated "Golden Cock" award—a literal translation from the Portuguese—for his original song, *Nobody Calls Me Prophet*. *Clean Up Woman* from 16-year-old Betty Wright of Miami, Florida, was such a great soul disc that Mick Jagger would name it as the record of the year. John Lennon was another notable booster of Betty Wright's record.

R & B had undergone much diversification since the mid-'60s. Like rock, it had spun off on many different tangents and produced some spectacular left-field hits. Jamaican reggae music had enjoyed huge popularity in Britain since the early '60s. The U.S. breakthrough came in '72, but it wasn't through the native variety of reggae performed by a Jimmy Cliff or a Prince Buster. It was a semi-established soul singer from Houston named Johnny Nash who brought reggae to the top of the American charts. Nash had scored a gold disc in '68 for *Hold Me Tight*, which had a faint reggae flavor. But by '72 he was able to reggae his way clear to the top of the charts with *I Can See Clearly Now*.

Sometimes it took the tenacity and endurance of a lone record promo man or a radio programmer or even a film producer to finally get a record to the top. Such a case was Roberta Flack's superb recording of *The First Time Ever I*

Rock had long since become big business with such dubious trappings as private jets, chauffered limos, entire hotel floors and $250,000 for a couple of hours on stage before the faithful. Few were better positioned to capitalize on rock's riches than the Stones, seen here still rolling on strong albeit in a private plane while the limos await their arrival at the next concert venue.

Historic moment in Edmonton, Canada as Procol Harum members rehearse with members of the city's symphony for a unique concert and live album

(Below) Paul McCartney, his family and backup group leave on a European tour

PRIME MINISTER · PREMIER MINISTRE

    Our contemporary music expresses in a unique, enjoyable, and often powerful way our ideas and emotions as a people. Knowing and appreciating our music enables us and music lovers from other countries to know Canadians better.

    I congratulate the members of Maple Music Inc., for organizing "The Maple Music Junket". Your efforts to expose European writers, editors, broadcasters, producers and film-makers to the contemporary music of Canada will, I am certain, result in exciting rewards.

    I am pleased to welcome to Canada our European visitors and wish them a happy and enjoyable visit.

Pierre Elliott Trudeau

Ottawa,
1972.

(Upper right) Canada's Pierre Trudeau rocks on with Ontario band Crowbar. (Lower right) Trudeau's letter promoting Maple Music to European media visitors (*credit: York*)
(Lower left) Britain's Marc Bolan

Saw Your Face. It took 2 full years before this single was finally broken into the charts. Because of its length and unusual style, radio stations feared it would be a tune-out factor. But after the song was featured in full in the Clint Eastwood movie, *Play Misty for Me*, Roberta Flack's smoother-than-silk revival of the Ewan McColl folk standard came to life all over the airwaves.

Experimentation had become part and parcel of the English rock scene in the '70s as bands endeavored to find unique approaches that would distinguish them from the musical mass. Several album-oriented acts, such as Yes, broke through into AM radio with singles that couldn't be denied. Some stations had been reluctant to program records that weren't familiar in commercial terms. But gradually the resistance wore down, and more and more album artists found that their music did indeed have a place on AM radio. As an increasing number of album groups sold millions of LPs and packed out football stadiums, Top 40 bent over backwards in an attempt to get their music onto AM playlists. And there was no doubt that this progressive music greatly enriched the sound of Top 40 radio.

One album act that crashed the singles barriers in '72 was the Moody Blues. They'd first scored in '65 with a cover version of the Bessie Banks R & B hit, *Go Now*. Late in the '60s, the Moodies moved into lush concept-album production and were immensely successful. Three years after the release of their first album, *Days of Future Passed*, a persistent deejay finally managed to break one of its finest tracks, *Nights in White Satin*.

An even more unlikely AM hit featured an allegedly "new" group called Derek and the Dominos. Actually the group was a long way from being new. The singing guitar player, Eric Clapton, who'd starred in the Yardbirds, Cream, and Blind Faith, had finally managed to overcome his lack of faith in his own vocal ability. Derek's rhythm section, the Dominos, consisted of Bobby Whitlock, Carl Radle, and Jim Gordon, plus, also on lead guitar, budding superstar guitar player, Duane "Skydog" Allman. Derek and the Dominos got together with a strong riff and a set of lyrics secretly concerned with Clapton's infatuation with George Harrison's wife, Patti Boyd. *Layla* was one of the longest hits in rock history.

America was a group of 4 Californian vocalists who moved to London trying to get together a recording deal. In '72 they wrote a mystical and metaphorical tune called *A Horse with No Name*, arranged it like a typical Neil Young number, and then watched it gallop to number one in both America and Britain.

Getting that big hit was never easy, not even for rock cult superstars such as Neil Young. Despite his near-legendary background with the Buffalo Springfield and Crosby, Stills, and Nash, not to mention 4 gold albums as a solo artist, it wasn't until the summer of '72 that Neil Young notched up his first million-selling single, and it was to be a beauty—from the *Harvest* album, *Heart of Gold*.

On the news front the tube was focused tightly on Nixon's historic junkets into Peking and Moscow. He and his high-profiled foreign affairs whiz, Henry Kissinger, wanted to open up new trade routes for U.S. corporations. Not even the Vietnam war, which had been a perennial thorn in Nixon's nerve centers, could hold back his desire to get to the trade bargaining table with the communists.

Among the most talented of the new crop of singer/song-writers was Jim Croce. His remarkable career would be meteoric, but cut tragically short by a plane crash. Croce scored a first-off gold single with the autobiographical tune, *You Don't Mess with Jim*.

Shortly after Nixon's foray into Peking, North Vietnam launched its spring offensive into the south. U.S. military advisers were so annoyed that they persuaded Nixon to allow them to mine the entrances to Haiphong harbor in an attempt to cut off supplies and military equipment from China.

Joining in the general rock trend of group splits, Paul Simon and Art Garfunkel parted company to pursue separate careers. Art would appear in the film of Joseph Heller's anti-war novel, *Catch 22*, while Paul would catch himself several notable hits. His desire for purity was most commendable. He traveled to Jamaica to capture an authentic reggae rhythm sound for his first smash hit as a solo artist, *Mother and Child Reunion*.

An equally gentle and wistful single was being put together by Jimmy Seals and Dash Crofts, 2 refugees from the '50s instrumental rock combo, the Champs. Rising up through the

Outstanding innovative singer/song-writer Don McLean (left) and Gilbert O'Sullivan, who created the classics *American Pie* and *Alone Again (Naturally)* respectively

folk circuit, they moved from coffee clubs to concert halls on the strength of their first hit single as a duo, a sensitive hot-weather ballad, *Summer Breeze*.

The world scene was still turbulent. Britain was forced to impose direct rule from Westminster on Northern Ireland in conflict between Catholics and Protestants. Both sides claimed to have God on their side, then proceeded to murder and maim hundreds of innocent bystanders in bomb explosions.

Elsewhere, revolutionary groups continued to create havoc with aircraft flights—the situation in which the technological world was at its most vulnerable. Despite intensified ground security, hijackings were still commonplace. At first neutral and left-wing nations had given permission to land hijacked aircraft, but mounting global pressure forced them to change policy.

In a terrorist attack on the Israeli section of Munich's Olympic Village, several Israeli Olympians were shot to death by Arab bandits. Other guerilla skyjackers held the world to ransom in order to obtain the release of the 3 surviving Olympics terrorists held by West Germany.

Assassins' bullets were flying again in the United States. On May 15, as he campaigned for the Democratic presidential nomination, George Wallace was gunned down by a would-be assassin, Arthur Bremer, who had been stalking the former Alabama governor for several months. Wallace survived the shooting, but there were doubts if he would ever be able to walk again.

Take It Easy was super summertime music from the Eagles, flying high with their first hit. The Eagles would go from strength to strength and ultimately wind up as one of America's most popular FM and AM artists. In '72 they took a song by singer/writer Jackson Browne, mixed in elements of the Beach Boys, Neil Young, and Crosby-Stills-Nash, and became the outstanding L.A. rock band of the new decade. It was an amazing achievement. Jackson Browne himself was enjoying the fruits of his first hit single, an outstanding original entitled *Doctor My Eyes*.

Meanwhile, up north in Canada history had been made in the previous November by the outstanding British band, Procol Harum, performing in concert with the Edmonton Symphony Orchestra. Involving more than 100 singers and musicians, the Edmonton concert was recorded and released in spring as *Procol Harum Live with the E.S.C.* It would be the first-ever gold album for the highly acclaimed classical rock group.

Canada was in world music news again in July with the Maple Music junket, a government-sponsored industry effort to turn on European media to the fast-emerging Canadian music scene. About 100 rock writers, deejays, editors, and commentators were flown to Canada to hear Maple Music at first hand. It was the first time that any government anywhere had officially backed rock music.

The year also brought a classic con story. A writer named Clifford Irving convinced a major book-publishing company, McGraw-Hill, to hand over a small fortune in cash for the rights to an authorized biography of the mysterious industrialist, Howard Hughes. It was later proved that Irving had never talked to Hughes; the manuscript was a complete fabrication.

As the '70s unfolded, more and more of us wanted to get back into the '50s and '60s. The future was like a nightmare. We dreamed of other times, when life seemd less confused and chaotic. We were tired of the endless warmongering and political manipulation. A folksinger/song-writer named Don McLean arrived at just the right time with an ode to the good old days of rock 'n' roll. His massive hit, *American Pie*, was dedicated to his idol, the great Buddy Holly.

In California, the self-proclaimed black revolutionary, Angela Davis, faced a death sentence on charges that she'd supplied weapons for the Soledad Brothers' prison escape attempt 2 years earlier. Two escapees were killed in the confusion of the escape, and one hostage was murdered. Right-wing elements in Washington were astounded when an all-white jury acquitted Ms. Davis on all charges.

Helen Reddy's *I Am Woman* demonstrated to the country that women really were standing up for their rights. Rock's relationship with female artists and audience had always been a tenuous affair. Rock was riddled with male chauvinism, so it was amazing to the record industry to find itself the vehicle for female protest.

One of the biggest records of the year came from a new British singer/song-writer who'd been named Gilbert O'Sullivan. His multimillion seller, *Alone Again (Naturally)*, won the hearts of parents and progeny alike. Cat Stevens, another British singer/song-writer, was an altogether different trip. An accomplished composer of sensitive songs, Stevens also had a knack of performing his music in unique style. He appealed to a broad cross-section of the populace, not just people who were into hard rock. Cat provided a perfect balance between ballads and big beat, as in the track from the *Tea for the Tillerman* album, *Morning Has Broken*.

One British artist who could consistently be relied upon to produce a fantastic live concert sound onstage was Elton John. Rapidly becoming one of the top draws in North America, Elton now appeared with a regular band comprising Dee Murray on bass, drummer Nigel Olsson, and guitarist Davey Johnstone. At the beginning of the year, Elton and his band had taken off for a French recording studio located in a mansion house with a splendid rural setting. They nicknamed the place "Honky Chateau" and proceeded to lay down an album that contained 2 smash hit singles — *Rocket Man* and *Honky Cat*.

Harry Nilsson, a Californian ex-bank clerk, had recorded material by many composers, but *Without You* was his own original, and a smash hit to boot.

By now the presidential campaign was all over the tube. In the early stages a lot of youthful hope was mustered behind the Democratic candidate, Senator George McGovern. He pursued the liberal vote, trying to seek rapport with alienated youth. McGovern was anti-war, anti-corporation-rape-of-our-natural resources, and, most important, anti-Nixon. He even suggested a form of socialism that appalled the system. The establishment responded by painting McGovern as an extreme and dangerous radical.

His campaign suffered a crushing blow when his just-appointed vice presidential running mate, Senator Thomas Eagleton, was forced to quit over documented reports of brief mental illness and unsubstantiated charges that he had an alcohol problem.

Nixon had chosen to run against radicalism, the revolutionary spirit, permissiveness, looser moral standards, and the counter-culture. Everything we stood for, Nixon was against, and vice versa. As Hurricane Agnes stormed across the eastern seaboard, leaving hundreds of thousands homeless in the worst floods of the century, the Nixon/Agnew political machine was sweeping the country. In the election, Dick Nixon creamed George McGovern by an all-time record margin. It was significant, though, that a staggering 62 per cent of the eligible American population had decided *not* to vote. Politics was passé.

OTHER NOTABLE RECORDS — '72

I GOTCHA — Joe Tex
LET'S STAY TOGETHER — Al Green
IF LOVING YOU IS WRONG — Luther Ingram
FAMILY AFFAIR — Sly and the Family Stone
OUTA SPACE — Bill Preston
OH GIRL — Chi-Lites
MY DING-A-LING — Chuck Berry
BANG A GONG — T. Rex
PAPA WAS A ROLLING STONE — Temptations
CONQUISTADOR — Procol Harum with the E.S.O.
ROUNDABOUT — Yes
LEAN ON ME — Bill Withers
SUNSHINE — Jonathan Edwards
STARTING ALL OVER AGAIN — Mel and Tim
HOLD YOUR HEAD UP — Argent
I SAW THE LIGHT — Todd Rundgren
VINCENT — Don McLean

1973

No longer did anyone doubt that Elton John would stop at nothing to gain attention. With stage outfits like this, he was sometimes hard to take seriously.

1973, and the music just kept rolling along, absorbing all sorts of outside influences and virtually erasing the MOR scene from the music business.

Chauvinism, or at least a yearning for a fast-disappearing past, had something to do with the astonishing popularity of John Denver. 1973 brought his second gold single, *Rocky Mountain High*, and helped establish him as one of the reigning superstars of the '70s.

Two of the hottest new female stars in North America shared one thing in common — both had been raised down under in Australia and had come to the northern hemisphere to seek fame and fortunes as singers. Olivia Newton-John had gone to London in '66 and emerged in the '70s with a string of countryish hits, including Bob Dylan's *If Not for You*, and *Banks of the Ohio*. Helen Reddy, another Aussie, had a number-one hit in '72 with *I Am Woman*. She dipped into the prodigious pot of southern songs for her second million-seller, *Delta Dawn*.

On the news scene, it finally appeared that the long and bitter Vietnam war was drawing to a close; on January 25 Nixon went on the tube to announce the end of hostilities. The chief architects of the Vietnam cease-fire agreement were Henry Kissinger and Hanoi's Le Duc Tho. For their efforts to bring about a settlement in this war-torn land, both men were awarded the 1973 Nobel Peace Prize. Tho refused it.

Predictably, it wasn't long before other global trouble spots began to fester. In Chile revolt broke out against the Marxist government of President Salvador Allende. A military junta seized control in a bloody overthrow, and Allende's bullet-spattered body was found in the palace. Some months later it would be revealed that one of America's largest corporations, ITT, had attempted to intervene in Chile's political evolution with bribes and illegal donations.

A few weeks later, student rioting in Greece led to a military coup that toppled Prime Minister Georgios Papadopolous.

In music, a new L.A. group called Steely Dan connected with the hit formula and sold a million copies of *Do It Again*. Steely Dan demonstrated the renewed importance of hit singles in the launching of new acts. Although most cities now had progressive FM stations, the alternative rock medium was no longer breaking new acts as it had in the late '60s. An AM single was once again a necessary prerequisite to success in the album market.

Space Oddity was a superb single by a new British superstar, David Bowie. It took several years to break the record, but it finally came through as a gold disc for England's glitter rock king — and queen, apparently. David Bowie was very big on bisexuality.

The environmental crisis continued to occupy young hearts and minds. Despite almost daily predictions of global catastrophes and severe shortages of natural resources, the system seemed to rumble on as before. Once again Detroit auto-makers were allowed to postpone the deadline for the installation of anti-pollution systems on new automobile models.

All sorts of superstars were writing flattering songs about one another in a sort of musical

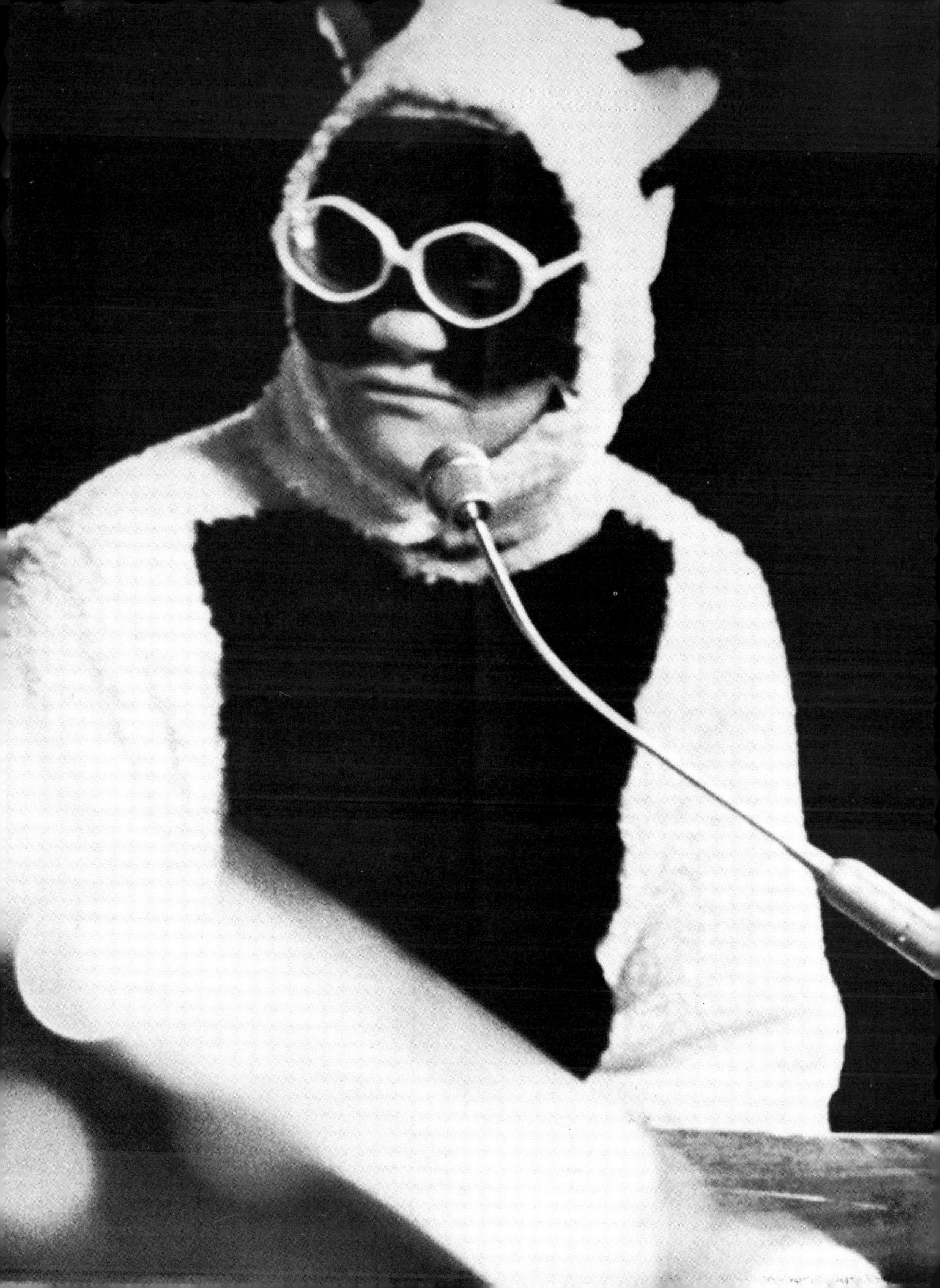

New rock superstars included:
(P. 158—upper left) David Bowie
(Upper right) Lou Reed
(Lower left) Jethro Tull's Ian Anderson
(Lower right) Carly Simon

(P. 159—upper left) Gregg Allman
(Upper right) Edward Bear's Larry Evoy
(Below left) Stevie Wonder
(Below right) Jim Croce

mutual admiration society. Eric Clapton had written *Layla* for George Harrison's wife, Patti Boyd. The Stones dedicated a new hit, *Angie*, to David Bowie's wife. And Carly Simon, a young woman who'd seen at least her share of the romantic action of recent times, penned a tune called *You're So Vain*: along the rock grapevine came the word that the song was about Mick Jagger.

From the LP, *Don't Shoot Me, I'm Only the Piano Player*, came a sixth gold smash for Elton John. *Crocodile Rock* demonstrated Elton's recognition of the roots of rock and a shrewd perception of a creeping wave of nostalgia. *Crocodile Rock* would snap its way to number one, to become Elton's first chart-topper.

Meanwhile, the wheels of war were turning again in the volatile Middle East. Russia had restocked the Arab arsenals in the years since the Six-Day War in '67, so that by '73 the Arabs felt sufficiently strong to risk a surprise attack. On October 6, the Jewish Yom Kippur, Syria and Egypt launched a strong offensive, taking the Israelis completely by surprise. The Arabs regained some of the territory lost in '67, but when the Israelis indicated they were about to launch a counter-offensive all the way to Cairo, a cease-fire was hastily arranged.

In the aftermath of the Yom Kippur War, the Arabs announced their possession of the most potent weapon of all: control of exports of their oil. America, as Israel's foremost supplier of military equipment, would be forced to endure skyrocketing prices for Arab oil.

The San Franciscan rock paper, *Rolling Stone*, had gone from strength to strength since its launching on the coat-tails of the Bay Area happening in '67. *Stone* now gave equal treatment to rock and to politics, a policy that seemed to bother some music freaks. By now other rock papers, such as *Cream*, *Zoo World*, *Phonograph Record*, *Circus*, and *Crawdaddy*, had sprung up to compete with *Stone* for record company advertising budgets.

By '73 the touchy issue of the American Indian was ready to explode. Like so many minority groups, native people were tired of being treated as third-class citizens. Indians had already occupied Alcatraz Island in an attempt to draw media attention to their condition. As the winter snows melted, bitter Indian militants took over Wounded Knee, South Dakota, where almost a century ago federal troops had massacred 200 Sioux men, women, and children. By manipulating media coverage, the Indians forced an uncaring government to take long-overdue steps to alleviate the appalling state of America's native people.

After his trip to Jamaica to record *Mother and Child Reunion*, Paul Simon had settled on Muscle Shoals, Alabama, as the site for his second album, *There Goes Rhymin' Simon*. *Kodachrome* seemed a sure-fire single hit, but then came hassles with the Kodak Corporation, owner of the Kodachrome trademark. Only after several days of bickering did the company's lawyers begin to understand what a fantastic free commercial for Kodachrome film the Simon record represented.

Ramblin' Man was the first hit single for America's most popular concert group, the Allman Brothers band. A light-hearted tune written by guitarist Richard Betts, it was featured on the Allmans' sixth album, *Brothers and Sisters*. (Their 5 earlier albums, all certified gold, had failed to yield an AM hit.) The Allmans had established their supremacy in '73 rock at the Watkins' Glen Rock Festival, where an estimated 600,000 music freaks turned out for an incredible gig featuring the Band, the Grateful Dead, and the Allmans. It was the biggest concert ever held.

Actually, the Allmans were no longer brothers since Duane "Skydog" Allman had died in a motorcycle accident in November '71. The only Allman left in the band, Gregg, began work on a long-overdue solo album. *Laid Back* was anything but laid back in its ascent of the charts, also yielding a great hit single in *Midnight Rider*.

The past was beginning to creep up on Richard Milhous Nixon. What the White House press secretary had originally dismissed as a "third-rate burglary" at the Democratic headquarters in Washington's Watergate Hotel was gradually becoming a national scandal.

By now undisputed as the most popular rock band in the world, Led Zeppelin returned in '73 with a historic tour and a fifth album, *Houses of the Holy*. During the 2½-month tour, Led Zeppelin would shatter many of the outdoor attendance records set by the Beatles at their peak. The tour was climaxed with a huge gig in Tampa, Florida, drawing almost 60,000 fans, the largest audience ever for a single concert act. The momentum of the tour also gave Led Zeppelin a big hit single, *D'Yer Mak'er*.

Sensational revelations and outrageous allegations were becoming commonplace as the modus operandi of the Nixon regime came under intense media scrutiny. Many large and studiously respectable corporations were to be charged with having made illegal and substantial contributions to the Nixon campaign warchest. American ambassadors were found to have bought their posts with hefty campaign donations. At all levels of American politics, there was a cancerous corruption that made the term "public interest" little more than a phrase tossed around by philosophers.

The man who'd made such a fuss about domestic dissenters and media criticism of White House conduct of the Vietnam war, vice president Spiro Agnew, pleaded no contest to charges of income-tax evasion and resigned his office. He avoided criminal action by copping a plea with the Justice Department and quitting his gig.

Deep Purple, a British album act, scored with *Smoke on the Water*, inspired by a real blaze that had destroyed the Montreux Casino in Switzerland after a peformance by Deep Purple and the Mothers of Invention at the Montreux Jazz Festival.

Since his revolutionary *What's Going On* album, and 4 gold hits, Marvin Gaye had moved out of the protest scene and back onto the rocky road of romance. *Let's Get It On* was a brilliant essay on a new morality that had gained much favor with the rock audience.

1973 was Motown's 13th year as a record company. One of its secrets of success was its knack of hanging onto its acts through thick and thin; very few artists had ever felt the need to leave Berry Gordy's stable. Mary "My Guy" Wells was one of the few acts to leave Motown in the '60s, and her career soon sank into obscurity. But by '72 the Four Tops had moved to Dunhill Records, Martha Reeves to MCA, and Gladys Knight and the Pips to Buddha. Gladys soon hit winning form with a Jim Weatherly tune, *Midnight Train to Georgia*. *Newsweek* magazine finally accorded Motown's musical genius, Stevie Wonder, a cover story. Stevie was then celebrating his 13th million-selling single, *Superstition*.

Love Train by the O'Jays provided another journey to the top of the charts for the red-hot Philly International label. Producers Kenny Gamble and Leon Huff were fast putting together a mini-Motown music complex—writing the songs, arranging the music charts, producing the records, and directing the promo efforts. It was virtually a hit production-line that hardly ever missed.

Sensing that standards of morality had changed radically since the moon-June-spoon era, Gamble and Huff used an unknown R & B vocalist named Billy Paul to produce a walkaway number-one smash with a song that not only admitted adultery was possible, but actually encouraged it—*Me and Mrs. Jones*.

Evidence of the new morality was all over contemporary culture. Movies were spiced and spliced with full frontal nudity, 4-letter words, oral copulation, and other no-no's of yesteryear. Magazines with blatant names such as *Screw* and *Gay* appeared on New York newsstands beside *Time* and *Business Week*. And nudity was no longer restricted to the female body. Now *Playgirl* magazine gained immense publicity by featuring a male nude centerspread utilizing celebrities who revealed their less well-known parts for big money.

In Hollywood, a composer named Lori Lieberman caught a Don McLean concert and was inspired to write a song using current slang called *Killing Me Softly with His Song*. While Ms. Lieberman's version went nowhere, Roberta Flack gave it her celebrated velvet touch and took the tune to number one.

Soul singer Dobie Gray, who'd set feet dancing in '65 with *The In Crowd*, got back in there himself in '73 with a powerful number called *Drift Away*. Most of us were to drift away a little ourselves, and no wonder. U.S. marijuana arrests hit a staggering total of 420,700 in '73, an increase of almost 130,000 over '72.

In Canada, a 3-piece Toronto band called Edward Bear (named after a Winnie the Pooh character), featuring singer/song-writer Larry Evoy, landed a million-seller with *Last Song*. And it would be the last song in the history of rock for '73.

OTHER NOTABLE RECORDS—'73

MY LOVE—Wings
STUCK IN THE MIDDLE WITH YOU—Stealer's Wheel
OH BABE WHAT CAN YOU SAY—Hurricane Smith
2001—Deodato
LIVING IN THE PAST—Jethro Tull
LISTEN TO THE MUSIC—Doobie Bros
DANIEL—Elton John
YOUR MAMA DON'T DANCE—Loggins and Messina
RIGHT PLACE WRONG TIME—Dr John
HIGHER GROUND—Stevie Wonder
A NATURAL HIGH—Bloodstone

1974

Gordon Lightfoot landed his first chart-topper with *Sundown* but the song was certainly no comment on his own blazing career

1974, the year of rock's 20th anniversary. It was, as the Righteous Brothers revival noted, a "rock 'n' roll heaven" as the music celebrated its completion of a second staggeringly successful decade.

Kung Fu Fighting was a massive '74 smash for Jamaican-born Carl Douglas. Although it wasn't quite the way Kung Fu was portrayed in the weekly TV series, Carl Douglas's record would sell over 3 million copies. It was his only hit, but with one-time sales like that, he could afford to do without a follow-up.

Stevie Wonder had never been so hot. He appeared on the children's TV series, *Sesame Street*, winning the hearts of the newest generation. And apart from maintaining his own spectacular recording career, he was writing hits for other acts. Aretha Franklin had sold a million of *Until You Come Back to Me*, and a group called Rufus scored with a Stevie Wonder song, *Tell Me Something Good*.

In the U.S.S.R. the dissenting novelist, Alexander Solzhenytsyn was arrested and then exiled from his homeland. And in the U.S. Dr. Timothy Leary, ex-Harvard professor and guru of psychedelia, was locked up in California having served one year of a 10-year sentence for being in a car where 2 marijuana roaches were found. In Texas, where the strictest grass laws were on the books, there was an automatic sentence of 2 years to life for possession of *any* quantity. A total or more than 700 young Texans were locked up for an average sentence of 9½ years on possession raps.

Although the dope laws remained totally repressive at a time when statistics had shown that more than 25 million Americans had smoked marijuana, change was in the air. The report on the National Commission of Marijuana and Drug Abuse had come out in favor of decriminalization of grass in '72. In '73 the state of Oregon had adopted a modified form of decriminalization.

October 20 was the night of the infamous Saturday Night Massacre. Nixon fired special Watergate prosecutor Archibald Cox, and in response, Attorney-General-designate Elliot Richardson and his deputy, William Ruckelshaus, resigned in protest. In its first editorial in over 50 years, the major weekly newsmagazine, *Time*, called for Nixon's resignation. Similar demands came in editorials by the *New York Times*, the *Detroit News*, and the *National Review*.

As successful as *Sundown* had been for Gordon Lightfoot, another Maple Music single would surpass all other records from around the world in total sales for '74. Terry Jacks' rendition of *Seasons in the Sun* would sell over 9 million copies, earning the Vancouver recluse more than one million dollars in record royalties alone.

Barry White, new soul-music star extraordinary, scored with *Can't Get Enough of Your Love*. And Paul Anka, the perennial pop singer, finally found the comeback smash he'd been seeking since the turn of the decade with *(You're) Having My Baby*. The song horrified the women's liberation movement, but Paul Anka could hardly care—the sales zoomed past the 2-million mark.

Lynnard Skynnard claimed that they'd named themselves after a high-school gym teacher who'd hassled them about their long hair. A 7-man band from Jacksonville, Florida, where the bullfrogs can croak in 3 octaves, Lynnard Skynnard came up with a great package of raunch and roll, *Sweet Home Alabama*, an answer to Neil Young's *Southern Man*.

From out of nowhere came Billy Swann and a song that brought back memories of the fab '50s.

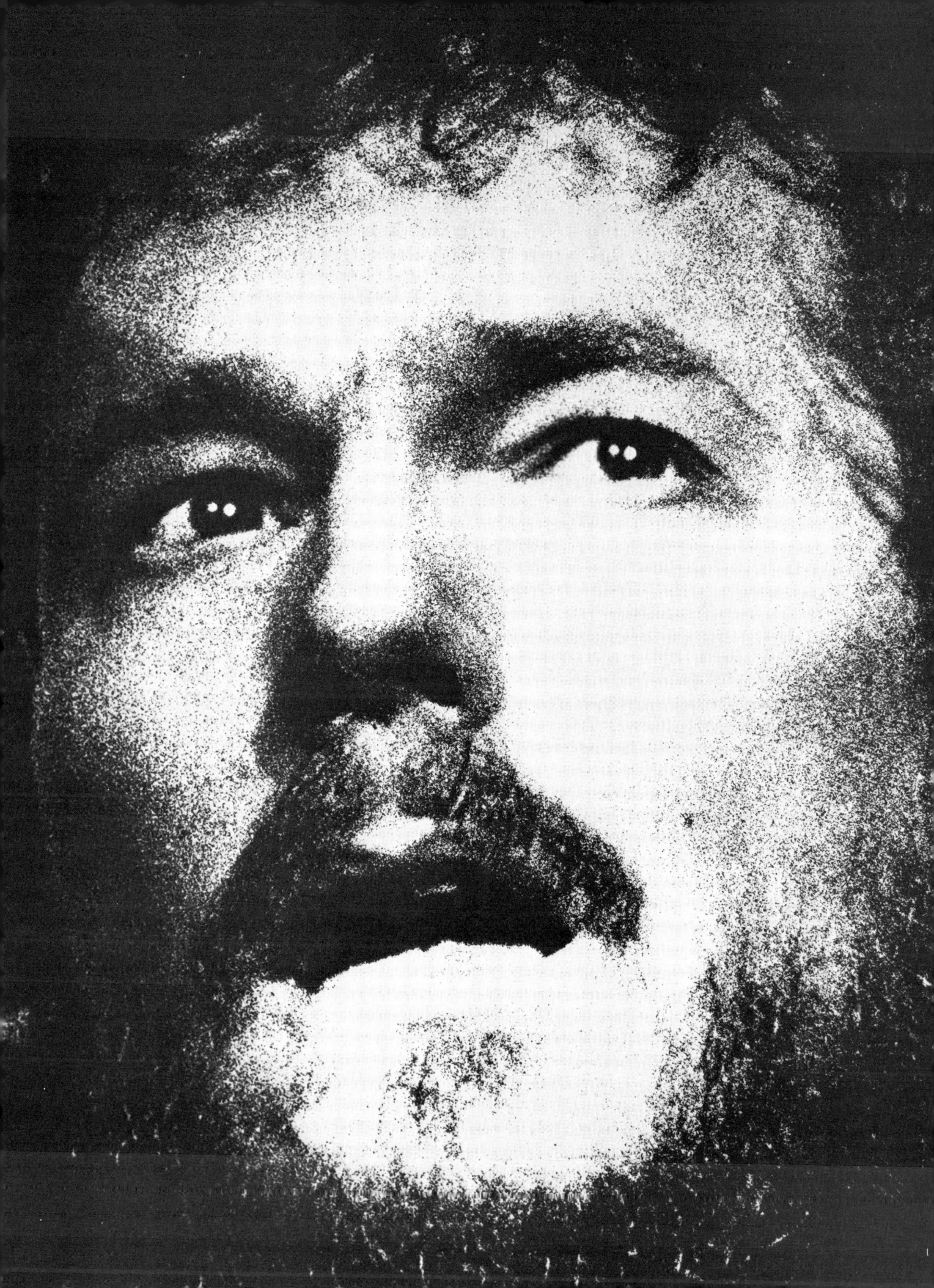

By now it was generally agreed that Elton John could outdraw any other single artist, a pudgy Presley included, anywhere on the planet

(P. 166—upper) John Lennon, getting his shit together in the Big Apple and glad to forget the other Apple
(Lower) By now Presley appeared an anachronism
(P. 167—upper) Like B.B. and Albert, Freddie King drew wide acclaim from blues enthusiasts but failed to crack the rock bigtime
(Lower) Eric Clapton made an overdue comeback with I Shot the Sheriff

Actually, Swann had been active in the '50s, co-writing the Clyde McPhatter million-seller, Lover Please. He moved on to Nashville and eventually took a gig playing guitar with Kris Kristofferson's band. Later came his chance to make a solo record, I Can Help, and it was a classic performance.

In the most sensational revelation of the torrid 2-year history of the Watergate affair, President Nixon finally admitted that he had been lying. Dick said he had known about the break-in 6 days after it had taken place and had actively tried to cover it up. What brought the truth rushing to the surface was a highly incriminating tape of a rap in Nixon's office about the break-in. Stunned by the contents of this tape, which destroyed all of Nixon's earlier claims of innocence, presidential counsel James St. Clair informed Nixon that he would resign unless the president made public the details.

In the aftermath of Nixon's disclosure about the June 23 tape, members of the Judiciary Committee in Congress revealed that they would vote for impeachment of the president. At 9:00 p.m. on August 9, President Nixon went on network TV to announce his resignation.

So the national nightmare was over, incoming President Ford soothed, with a sigh of relief. Time to get it out of the way so that the nation could get back to business. But to young people, the nightmare was only just beginning as we faced the horrors of a planet in drastic turmoil. Amidst the current political chaos, the Hues Corporation could not have been better named. The 3 members combined perfectly on the '74 million-seller *Rock the Boat* from the album, *Freedom for the Stallion*.

The '60s had brought profoundly depressing and complex questions about the so-called good life, which supposedly depended on vertical economic growth and prosperity and on traditional morals and values. Middle America, which had given Nixon its whole-hearted endorsement in '72, had hoped that Dick would whip the trouble-makers — noisy radicals, hippies, and blacks. And now came the irony of his own expulsion.

Hard rock was happening hot and heavy in '74, and there could be little doubt that the most important discoveries of the year were Bachman-Turner Overdrive and Britain's Bad Company. Ex-Guess Who guitarist Randy Bachman formed BTO after an earlier band, Brave Belt, had failed to get off the ground. Finding the word "overdrive" in a magazine for truck drivers, the devout Mormon musician put it all together as BTO. Their first album yielded a smash single, *Blue Collar Worker*. *BTO II* brought forth a second gold single, *Takin' Care of Business*, another Randy Bachman original.

Can't Get Enough was a convenient theme song for the hot new British band, Bad Company. There was nothing particularly progressive or avant garde about the music of either Bad Company or BTO, but both gained enormous followings in '74. Bad Company, comprising former members of Free and Mott the Hoople, were promoted under the shrewd guidance of Led Zeppelin's new Swan Song label. With the first single and album from Swan Song, Bad Company ended up at number one on both charts.

Don't Let the Sun Go Down on Me was another number-one smash for Elton John. And you can believe that nobody in the record industry was going to let the sun go down on Elton's career, least of all concert promoters and record retailers. Elton's popularity had soared to enormous heights as he undertook the longest U.S. tour any British act had tried on in the '70s. And for once, quality endured over quantity. *Don't Let the Sun Go Down on Me* was recorded during a month-long session at the Caribou Studios in Colorado. The resulting *Caribou* album was another platinum seller for Elton, confirming the shrewd reasoning of MCA Records. MCA had recently signed a new contract with Elton, reported to be the most lucrative in the history of the record business. The contract guaranteed him a minimum of $8.5 million over 5 years.

Later in the year Elton revived the Beatles' classic from *Sgt. Pepper*, *Lucy in the Sky with Diamonds*. He was even shrewd enough to ensure critical support for *Lucy* by flying its composer, John Lennon, into the Caribou studios to sing harmony vocals. It was a highly credible endorsement for Elton. Fast becoming rock's most visible socialite, Elton returned Lennon's favor by providing studio assistance and promotion support on the new hit Lennon single, *Whatever Gets You Through the Night*.

After shaking off a 2-year affair with heroin, Eric Clapton flew to Miami to cut a comeback album named after the address of the studio, *461 Ocean Boulevard*. They might have been short of title ideas, but the music was as fine as ever. Eric then launched into a lengthy North American tour, performing old songs, new songs, and even a few borrowed and blue tunes. His guitar playing, when he let himself cut loose, was as fluid and as fascinating as his best days with Cream and Blind Faith. His sensational comeback single, *I Shot the Sheriff*, wasn't really an oldie; the tune was an original by a Jamaican reggae group called Bob Marley and the Wailers, who really lived up to their name.

On the lighter side, Sly Stone was married on the Madison Square Garden stage in a glittering celebrity ceremony, while J. Geils band singer, Peter Wolf, and long-time lady friend, actress Faye Dunaway, were married in a somewhat more sedate setting in Beverly Hills, the new turf of heavy rock stars. It all reflected the growing acceptance of the cultural and economic domination of entertainment by rock music.

OTHER NOTABLE RECORDS — '74
BAND ON THE RUN — Wings
MIDNIGHT AT THE OASIS — Maria Muldaur
FEEL LIKE MAKIN' LOVE — Roberta Flack
THE JOKER — Steve Miller
ROCK YOUR BABY — George McRae
RADAR LOVE — Golden Earring
YOU AIN'T SEEN NOTHIN' YET — B.T.O.
THE SHOW MUST GO ON — Leo Sayer
CAT'S IN THE CRADLE — Harry Chapin
TIN MAN — America
BOOGIE DOWN — Eddie Kendricks
I'VE GOT THE MUSIC IN ME — Kiki Dee

1975

1975—the mid-period of the soaring '70s and it really did seem as if everything was soaring higher than ever before, especially in the area of inflation. After moaning about rising costs, the oil companies later announced record profits and burned up yet more of their sagging corporate credibility.

To some observers, the music scene was stagnating under the weight of radio programming restrictions. It had become, many critics claimed, a kind of Mod Muzak. Whatever the reason, there seemed to be a lack of significant new stars on the rise.

The only bright spot in the exposure of fresh talent came from the revived disco boom.

Singer Carol Douglas, taking *Doctor's Orders,* set the dancing pace for '75's disco generation. The discos were back and setting musical trends; radio stations were playing more records in the dancing groove. Eight years after the '67 death of dancing, people were getting up and getting it on again . . . and often with other people.

The demand for disco records was moving into uptempo as the music industry sniffed out a definite trend in audience tastes. And so the disco bandwagon came into being.

That's the Way I Like It was a hit for KC and the Sunshine Band, an anonymous group from Florida taking advantage of the need for faceless and imageless stars in the disco scene. The demand for disco records opened the doors to many unknown performers and created an outbreak of new talent on AM airwaves. And that's the way fans like it, as KC and the Sunshine Band came through with the top disco hit of the year, *Get Down Tonight.*

But it wasn't all unknowns making big disco noise in the mid-70s . . . also prominent were several new-wave "freaky" R & B vocal groups who jumped aboard the disco train and rode it to the top. This included the Funkadelic, Tower of Power and from the heart of the Midwest, Chicago's Ohio Players, rocking up a storm with *Fire*.

Never Can Say Goodbye, the Jackson 5's Motown hit of '71, was brought up to date in sizzling disco style by one of several new female singers who bounced into the scene in '75 . . . along with LaBelle, Minnie Riperton, Shirley and Company, Janis Ian, Linda Ronstadt and Melissa Manchester. Rock had long been a male chauvinist endeavor, but gradually the ladies were getting in there and holding their own. And not only on vinyl . . . .

The daily news reports were filled with female headlines—in Britain, the stoutly male Conservative Party abandoned all good-old-chap traditions and voted a woman, Mrs. Margaret Thatcher, as its new leader, replacing Edward Heath.

In America, Jackie Kennedy became a widow once again with the death of her second husband, the Greek shipping magnate, Aristotle Onassis.

Linda Ronstadt did up an old Everly Brothers tune from 1960, *When Will I Be Loved*. Since teaming up with a new producer, Peter Asher of Peter and Gordon fame, Ms. Ronstadt hadn't put a disc out of place. Like Ms. Ronstadt, Patti LaBelle made a notable comeback in '75. Thirteen years earlier, Pattie LaBelle and her BlueBelles had scored with *I Sold My Heart to the Junkman.* Working with the famed New Orleans producer/song-writer, Allen Touissant, LaBelle tore up the charts with *Lady Marmalade.*

Another lady in the news was newspaper heiress Patty Hearst who was finally tracked down and captured by the FBI in September. Two other American women were to see the inside of a courtroom through alleged assassination attempts on President Ford—in Sacramento, Lynette Fromme pointed a loaded

Losing his hair and his artistic credibility, Elton John (left) hung on grimly but his best songs seemed in the past
Olivia Newton-John (right) sprung from down under but soon reached the top
Linda Rondstadt (below) finally connected with a hit streak through the perception of her producer, Peter Asher, of Peter and Gordon fame.

(Above left) Lynyrd Skynnard, a Southern band, hit paydirt with *Sweet Home Alabama,* an answer song to Neil Young's *Southern Man*
(Below) The dying moments of Canada's highly successful Guess Who as singer/keyboards player Burton Cummings (left) listens to guitarist Dom Troiano expound his rock philosophy
(Above right) Barry White offered black silk and soda soul

gun at the President; and in San Francisco, where Sara Jane Moore fired and missed. Gerry Ford vowed that such attempts would not keep him off American streets.

In the rock scene, the original *Society's Child*, Janis Ian, bobbed up with her first hit since 1967, the sensitive ballad, *At 17.*

The biggest movie blockbuster of the year — the film which would quickly go on to surpass *Gone With the Wind* and *The Sound of Music* as top-grossing movie of all time — was *Jaws*. Based on a novel by Peter Benchley, Jaws was an old-fashioned fear-and-phobia exploitation film. The movies were doing their darndest to regain some of the vast audience which had turned on to rock music as the prime source of '70s entertainment. But the music business just kept on getting bigger and bigger, setting the scene for a perfect piece of parody by Sugarloaf... *Don't Call Us (We'll Call You).*

It was obvious to all that rock had become big business, overflowing with big bucks. *Forbes*, the prominent U.S. business magazine, pointed out that the annual dollar gross of rock music was greater than the *combined* earnings of the movie, TV and professional sports businesses. Rock music had become, claimed *Forbes* magazine, the last bastion of the American Dream, the only remaining endeavor where fortunes could be made and lost overnight.

Elton John, *the* superstar of the mid-'70s, scored the first hit which he had not written himself — John Lennon's *Lucy in the Sky with Diamonds*. Only Elton would have had the audacity to tackle one of the Beatles' most highly acclaimed tunes, among the finest highlights of the brilliant Sgt. Pepper album. Not only that, Elton managed to persuade John Lennon to sing harmony on the new version, adding much to its artistic stature. Elton later repaid the favor by singing on John Lennon's first chart-topper in many, many months — *Whatever Gets You Through the Night.*

Elton, in fact, had become the New Beatles. But he had not forgotten his humble beginnings. The new album, *Captain Fantastic and the Brown Dirt Cowboy,* was a musical autobiography of the rise to fame and fortune of Elton and his lyricist, Bernie Taupin.

By now fame and fortune had taken over the direction of Elton's life. He was a highly visible superstar, the most accessible top rock act of the '70s. Elton even agreed to take part in the movie production of the Who's highly rated rock opera, *Tommy*, along with a host of superstars including the Who, Ringo Starr, Eric Clapton and Ike and Tina Turner. Yet another chart-topper would come Elton's way before the year was out... the hard-rocking *Philadelphia Freedom*. Throughout '75, Elton John maintained a very high profile... overshadowing even the master headline-maker, Mr. Bisexuality himself, David Bowie. Changing his image as rapidly as oil prices went up, Bowie demonstrated his cynicism about rock 'n' roll bigtime in the song he wrote and recorded with everyone's friend, John Ono Lennon... *Fame.*

Neil Sedaka was the comeback story of the year in Rock '75, and the second of two million-sellers, *Bad Blood*, featuring harmony vocals from Neil's record company owner, Elton John, president of Rocket Records. It was Sedaka's first chart-topper since *Breaking Up Is Hard to Do* from '62 and his eighth gold single. 1975 was a fantastic year for Sedaka — not content with two gold hits of his own — *Laughter in the Rain* and *Bad Blood* — he also wrote one of the year's top songs by a new act named Captain and Tenille... *Love Will Keep Us Together*.

There was no shortage of bad blood in southeast Asia where American forces were hastily evacuated as South Vietnam surrendered unconditionally to the Viet Cong. Thus ended one of the least glorious endeavors of American history... leaving an unwon war in Vietnam and a split culture at home. On top of the horrors of the Nixon regime, the emergency mass airlift out of Saigon was almost too much to bear.

On the crime front, Montreal firemen discovered thirteen bodies in the burnt-out remains of the Gargantua Bar/Salon which had been torched by Mob heavies. In Detroit, controversial union figure and former Teamsters' president, Jimmy Hoffa, disappeared and police suspect he was the victim of a mysterious gangland slaying. Seagrams whisky heir, Samuel Bronfman, was kidnapped with an asking ransom of $2.3 million. Later he and the money were located and the two kidnappers marched off to jail. And London again was the scene of scores of despicable IRA bombings.

The Bee Gees thundered back on the hit trail after a couple of years' absence with the first of several hits produced by veteran Atlantic Records' arranger/producer, Arif Mardin... *Jive Talkin'*. Mardin, who was given a Grammy as Record Producer of the Year '75, had first risen to prominence for his work with Aretha Franklin in the late '60s. The Bee Gees' followup was another gold smash, *Nights on Broadway*. It was another highly successful year for Redcoat rock 'n' rollers... now in its 12th year, the British invasion blazed on without letup. A highly rated group of London session musicians collectively known as 10 CC found the single they'd been seeking with *I'm Not in Love*, from an album entitled *The Original Soundtrack*..

Now emerging as America's most popular homegrown group, the ever-commercial Eagles flew high with *The Best of My Love*, a smash hit from their *On the Border* album. As the year drew to a close, it had become apparent that a softer West Coast-country harmony sound was emerging with hits from the Eagles, Linda Ronstadt, and others.

The heady activism of the '60s was barely a memory as an avalanche of apathy had buried the rock 'n' roll generation. Forgetting-the-present had become *the* national pastime of not only the rock generations but all generations. Depression fears clogged American media as the economy took a steep downturn in the aftermath of the oil squeeze. Jobs were harder to get. Basic, gut issues were coming into political focus but most of us simply turned away from it. Somehow it was *their* problem, not ours. Not yet anyway.

British music had maintained a strong hold on American charts. Elton John remained the single most popular rock entertainer in the world, while Led Zeppelin continued to be the globe's most popular rock group. Their '75 album *Physical Graffiti*, reached number one on the album charts faster than any album in history. Predictably it produced no hit singles.

And thus rock 'n' roll, now in its 21st year, had not only survived but had billowed out into the most successful entertainment medium of the century, in dollar terms. Rock had become big business, the biggest there is in show biz. The huge financial rewards may have had something to do with the reclusive lifestyles adopted by so many of rock's superstars. Wherever goes big money, Confucius might have said, goes big hassles too. Whatever the reason, people seemed to be having less fun making rock 'n' roll. The directions were hard to chart as 1976 rolled around along with the American Bicentennial. To some observers, it appeared that rock music was about to enter a new cycle. In its first 21 years, rock 'n' roll had traveled many roads in many directions, and had grown stronger for the experience..

OTHER NOTABLE RECORDS — '75
SISTER GOLDEN HAIR — America
LOVING YOU — Minnie Riperton
WHY CAN'T WE BE FRIENDS — War
YOU ARE SO BEAUTIFUL — Joe Cocker
BUNGLE IN THE JUNGLE — Jethro Tull
FEELINGS — Morris Albert
PICK UP THE PIECES — A. W. B.
BOOGIE ON REGGAE WOMAN — Stevie Wonder